# SOCIAL ORGANIZATION AND CULTURAL AESTHETICS

*Essays in Honor of William H. Davenport*

Edited by

**William W. Donner**
**James G. Flanagan**

University Press of America, Inc.
Lanham • New York • Oxford

Copyright © 1997 by
**University Press of America,® Inc.**
4720 Boston Way
Lanham, Maryland 20706

12 Hid's Copse Rd.
Cummor Hill, Oxford OX2 9JJ

All rights reserved
Printed in the United States of America
British Library Cataloguing in Publication Information Available

**Library of Congress Cataloging-in-Publication Data**

Social organization and cultural aesthetics : essays in honor of William
H. Davenport / edited by William W. Donner and James G. Flanagan.
p. cm.
Includes bibliographical references.
1. Ethnology. 2. Ethnology--Oceania. 3. Oceania--Social life and
customs. 4. Davenport, William H., 1922-. I. Davenport, William H.,
1922. II. Donner, William Wilkinson. III. Flanagan, James G., 1949.
GN325.S62  1997   305.8'00995--dc21    97-19969 CIP

ISBN 0-7618-0783-7 (cloth: alk. ppr.)
ISBN 0-7618-0784-5 (pbk: alk. ppr.)

∞™ The paper used in this publication meets the minimum
requirements of American National Standard for information
Sciences—Permanence of Paper for Printed Library Materials,
ANSI Z39.48—1984

# Contents

| | |
|---|---|
| Acknowledgments | v |
| Introduction<br>*James G. Flanagan and William W. Donner* | 1 |
| W.H. Davenport: Principal Works | 13 |
| Missionary Ventures in Hawaii:<br>19th Century Wives, 20th Century Social Workers<br>*Judith Modell* | 19 |
| Empowered Women<br>*Laura Zimmer-Tamakoshi* | 45 |
| Exchanging Sisters Is Not a Game<br>*James G. Flanagan* | 61 |
| Kinship and Social Organization:<br>Traditional Issues in the Study of Modernity<br>*William W. Donner* | 73 |
| *Resepsi:* Dou Donggo Wedding Receptions<br>as Cultural Critique<br>*Peter Just* | 95 |

Chiefs Who Fall Down and Get Washed Out to Sea:
The Limitation of Museum Objects in the Representation of
Ethnographic Reality
*Miriam Kahn* 113

Affect and Paradox in Museum Exhibits
*Peter H. Welsh* 129

## Acknowledgments

The editors wish to thank the Department of Anthropology at the University of Pennsylvania and the University of Pennsylvania Museum of Archaeology and Anthropology for their support of this project. We especially want to thank Igor Kopytoff who oversaw the production of this book, and Jennifer Quick who edited it.

# Introduction

*James G. Flanagan and William W. Donner*

**A Personal Portrait**

It is a difficult task to summarize the influence of someone who has such rich and diverse interests and abilities. Bill Davenport's special genius is to command this abundance, and at the same time be able to summon the sharp focus needed for good scholarship. For all his range of experience and knowledge, he controls details. The result is a scholar who has produced a series of seminal articles in a variety of different areas and who also has inspired his students with the excitement of anthropology.

Bill Davenport's interests cut across academic boundaries. Before studying anthropology, he learned commercial art and photography, worked in the Merchant Marine, and served in World War II. He studied anthropology at the University of Hawaii and Yale. He later taught at Yale, the University of Pennsylvania, Bryn Mawr College, the University of California at Santa Cruz, and the University of Hawaii. He was raised on the West Coast, held most of his academic positions on the East Coast, and did most of his field research in the Pacific. He has done ethnographic research in Indonesia, Malaysia, Solomon Islands, Hawaii, and Jamaica. As a graduate student he participated in an interdisciplinary program in human relations at Yale. He has published in journals as diverse as *American Anthropologist, Journal of the Polynesian Society, Baessler-Archiv, Journal of American Folklore, Scientific American* and *Expedition*. He has published significant papers on a wide variety of topics, including social organization, art, game theory, sexuality, economics, leadership, and culture change. Throughout his career he has maintained an academic interest in fields which seem disparate—art and social organization. He was on the board at the Bishop Museum and a director at the Smithsonian, and served on many committees of the American Anthropological Association. This range of experiences, a curator's attention to detail, an original mind, an ability to relate to other humans, and sheer enthusiasm for his work account for Bill's special genius as a scholar and teacher.

Bill grew up in Cucamonga, California, then a small agricultural community. Before graduating from high school, he spent a year working on merchant ships, an experience which reinforced a lifelong love of the sea and sailing. After graduating from high school, he attended the Art Center School and learned photography. During this time he also worked as a commercial photographer for Lockheed and then in the studios at Technicolor and Fox. He moved to Hawaii and took over a photography business. During World War II, he served in the navy's merchant marine, transporting troops and supplies. It was during this time that he first traveled to the Solomon Islands, unloading supplies at Lunnga River in Guadalcanal; he later served in New Guinea.

After the war, he went to Shanghai, China, and trained Chinese in operating new vessels. He left as the revolution engulfed China. When he returned to Hawaii, he formed a partnership with several others to run a freight ship between Samoa, Tahiti, and Hawaii. A few years later, already in his mid-twenties, he began undergraduate studies at the University of Hawaii. His original interest was in Asian philosophy, especially in Japan and China, but he then became interested in anthropology. He worked as a photographer with Peter Buck and Kenneth Emory at the Bishop Museum and eventually majored in anthropology. He studied with Leonard Mason, Katharine Luomala, and Saul Riesenberg at the University of Hawaii. Even in his senior year, he was still undecided about whether he would go to graduate school in anthropology or philosophy.

He chose anthropology at Yale University. Buck had taught there and both Emory and Mason had attended Yale. In his second year at Yale, he received a Ford foundation grant to participate in an interdisciplinary study in behavioral sciences. In addition to anthropology, he took courses in behavioral psychology, psychoanalytic techniques, statistics, and sociological theory. He studied or worked with scholars from a variety of disciplines, including John Dollard and John Hollingshead. He took anthropology courses from Ralph Linton, Peter Murdock, Floyd Lounsbury, Ben Rouse, and Sidney Mintz. The program, which combined modified psychoanalytic theory with Hull's behaviorism, gave him a broad academic background which included training in psychological testing methods and exposure to sociological theory, in addition to anthropology. He obtained his Ph.D. from Yale in 1956 for a dissertation entitled *A Comparative Study of Two Jamaican Fishing Communities.*

He taught in the anthropology department at Yale University from 1955 to 1958 and 1960 to 1963. There he also participated in the Tri-Institute Pacific Program. This project was an alliance between the Bishop Museum, Yale University, and the University of Hawaii to identify areas of the Pacific for anthropological research. Bill became interested in Santa Cruz in the Solomon Islands and did two and a half years of research there.

He began working at the University of Pennsylvania in 1963, as an associate curator in the University Museum. In 1967 he was promoted to professor in anthropology and was made a curator in the Museum. For the next twenty-five years he stayed primarily at the University of Pennsylvania, although he also taught at the University of California at Santa Cruz (1969–1972), Bryn Mawr College (1967, 1973), and the University of Hawaii (1976).

He returned to the Solomon Islands for twenty-one months from 1964 to 1966 to conduct research in the Central and Eastern Districts (now Central and Temotu Provinces), for three months in 1974, and again in 1976.

He also developed an interest in the ethnography of Southeast Asia, and went to Maluku, Indonesia, in 1974 and then South Sulawesi, Indonesia, in 1985. Starting in 1990 and continuing until the present (1994), he has been conducting field research in Sarawak, Malaysia. He worked as an advisor to the Ford Foundation project in Southeast Asia, helping to train local scholars and curators in managing research and museum projects.

Throughout this time he maintained an abiding interest in Hawaiian culture. He published a book on Hawaiian art (1974, 1988c), and an article on Hawaiian political organization (1969b). He also did research on the genealogies of Hawaiian royalty which has recently been published (1994).

He made important service contributions to the profession. He was an associate of the Bernice P. Bishop Museum from 1953 to 1960 and from 1980 to the present. He was a Fellow at the Center for Advanced Study in the Behavioral Sciences from 1971 to 1972. He worked as a consultant for the Ford Foundation in East Malaysia in 1974. He was a member of the Smithsonian Council from 1976 to 1984. He also served on the American Anthropological Association's special committee to investigate research activities in Thailand during an especially difficult time in the Association's history. He is a Fellow in the American Anthropological Association, the American Association for the Advancement of Science, American Ethnological Society, and an Honorary Fellow of the Association of Social Anthropologists in Oceania.

It is not possible to place Bill within any specific anthropological school or approach; indeed, he is especially inspiring because of his diversity and range of interests. But to the contributors to this volume, he represents a generation of anthropologists which was significantly different from our own. He started in anthropology at a time when professional networks were dense: there were few anthropologists and everyone knew everyone. Fieldwork was done in small-scale foreign communities. These communities appeared to be relatively self-contained and self-sufficient. There were many debates in anthropology but also a generally agreed upon body of shared knowledge which constituted the core of the discipline. At the least, people agreed upon what they were disagreeing about. There was still the assumption that anthropology could be developed into an empirical science. The students who contributed to this volume live in a different world. There is no longer a body of knowledge which everyone agrees upon as essential for an anthropologist to know. Many anthropologists now study in Western societies and most who do fieldwork in small-scale foreign cultures find them radically affected by a world system.

The diversity of Bill's interests formed a scholar able to discuss a variety of topics with his students. He is well versed in anthropology, but also knows philosophy, art, social psychology, and social theory. He has extensive field experience throughout the Pacific yet he first visited the region before he was an anthropologist. He can discuss Polynesian migrations, then refer to his own experiences in sailing and navigation. He can discuss the aesthetics of non-Western art, connect that with his personal experience as a commercial photographer, and further bring to bear his training as a philosopher. He can discuss contemporary Hawaiian politics as an anthropologist who is familiar with Hawaiian ethnology and also as someone who came to Hawaii before World War II, lived and worked there for fifteen years, and has made frequent visits since.

But perhaps most surprising for a scholar commanding this span of interests and possessing such a creative, original mind, he can also command details across a range of topics. In managing the Museum's collections, he is an old-fashioned curator who knows the collections intimately and literally as material culture. He has an eye for recognizing techniques of manufacture and the significance of the material and method used in manufacture. At the same time, this attention to material details is parallelled by his command of academic details. In his classes, he discusses not only the mechanics of manufacturing artifacts but also various philosophical theories of aesthetic production and representation.

Finally, perhaps because of his life before academia, he has an unusual sensitivity to others. He was supportive of a variety of different students, often with quite varying interests. Whereas other influential scholars of his generation developed theoretical frameworks, Bill's sensitivity provided insights about human behavior which transcend the limitations of a particular approach. The theoretical frameworks developed by many of his teachers and his contemporaries have been found to be lacking; much of contemporary theory calls into question the faith that cultural anthropology can be developed into an empirical and scientific discipline. But inherent in Bill's sensitivity to others is a kind of Malinowskian empiricism of understanding others by living with them. Bill's ability to connect with people, both to understand the cultures of the people he lived with and to explain those cultures to his students, reflects an empiricism which claims that learning about cultural behavior is both possible and exciting.

## An Intellectual Portrait

In the foregoing, brief personal portrait we have tried to convey part of Bill Davenport's contribution to anthropology through his direct contact with others. In particular, we have mentioned that the breath of his personal experience coupled with his infectious enthusiasm for the discipline and for the "ethnographic world" remain as parts of a lasting legacy in the minds of all those who had the privilege of working with him. Beyond that, however, these same characteristics contribute directly to his anthropology.

To one unfamiliar with the man, the appearance in 1972 of "Preliminary Archaeological Excavations in the Eastern Solomon Islands," harking back as it does to an almost Boasian involvement with all subdisciplines, would come as a surprise. The discipline has now become far too specialized for such eclecticism. But house sites, spears, settlement patterns, kinship terminologies, folktales, male initiation rituals, and sculptures are all cultural artifacts. Anthropology is concerned with the analysis of these artifacts in full recognition of the socio-cultural contexts in which they are located and the individual initiative involved in their production and reproduction.

But breadth of interest in Davenport's case is not bought at the cost of depth of ethnographic knowledge. This is nowhere more evident than in the series of papers on Santa Cruz social organization (1964d, 1968b, 1968c, 1969b, 1972b). Based on two years of fieldwork, conducted between 1958 and 1960, here is as fine, and as fine-grained, an analysis of social organization as we have for any Pacific Island group.

Davenport's interest in social organization was initially manifest in his paper "Non-Unilinear Descent and Descent Groups" (1959c). Here, developing upon Goodenough's distinction between *kindreds*, as being composed of persons related within a specified degree of collaterality to a particular individual, and *descent groups*, as being composed of persons who trace their relationship lineally through either or both sexes to a known or unknown ancestor, he presents the structural features which in their various combinations produce the variety of kin groupings we find in the ethnographic record. The importance of this paper and the recognition that Davenport was emerging as a significant voice in social organization studies is evident in the fact that he was invited to contribute the chapter on "Social Structure" in LeBar and Suddard (1960b) and the chapter on "Social Organization" in the 1963 *Biennial Review of Anthropology* (1963). The extended series of publications on Santa Cruz social structure and social organization, then, is to be seen as an integral aspect of Davenport's vision of anthropology. Unfortunately, because of their publication in the European *Baessler-Archiv* these papers are not as accessible to American anthropologists as one might like. The initial paper (Davenport 1964e) dealing with the main island of Santa Cruz (Nidu), while presenting the major organizational features, settlement and domestic groups, marriage, kinship terminology, descent and political organizations, once again emphasizes the interrelationship of individual and society. Davenport concludes that as one example of the emergence of leaders in so-called stateless societies, Nidu presents an "instance where structural and psychological analyses, thought to be irrelevant to each other by many anthropologists, become highly related" (1964:91).

Two further papers on Santa Cruz social organization appeared in 1968. The first deals with the islands of the extreme northeast, known as the Duff Islands or Taumako. The second deals with the two southeastern island groups, Utupua and Vanikoro. Davenport is concerned to demonstrate the great cultural and linguistic diversity that exists in the Santa Cruz group. The six and one half thousand Santa Cruz Islanders speak eight different indigenous languages. Although Taumako is actually a Polynesian Outlier, the inhabitants share many more cultural features with their neighbors than with Polynesian societies to the east. The paper is a marvelous demonstration of how productive attention to the details of settlement can be in understanding traditional societies (1968b:148–57). In contrast, the Utupuans and Vanikoroans fit much more easily than the Taumakoans into a standard Melanesian model. Utupua provides the main focus of the paper. On Utupua, people are aligned into a "number of exogamous matrilineal descent groups" (1968c:220), residence is "invariably virilocal" (1968c:217), and the "formal social organization of the men's house association is the same thing as the local political organization" (1968c:222). The dynamic of Utupuan society is provided by the tension between matrilineages which are "landholding and exogamous social categories" and men's house associations whose continuity is provided by "agnatic succession" and which is "representative of the localized residential group only," not the dispersed lineages (1968c:230).

In 1969 Davenport presented the broad organizational features of the Main Reef Islands (1969a), the group in most intensive cultural and economic contact with the main island of Nidu (here called Nede; 1969a:153ff). As elsewhere on Santa Cruz, individual nuclear families constitute the majority of households and "the individual household stands out clearly as the basic social unit" (1969a:172). The densely populated Main Reef Islands "have never been and are not now self-sufficient" in terms of subsistence (1969a:174). Imports of subsistence goods were paid for by the export of women, both as wives and concubines, to the main island of Nede whose men paid heavy bride and purchase prices in red feather money (1969a:174). While descent is matrilineal, a distinction is maintained between a wife (whose children affiliate with their matrilineage) and a concubine (whose children affiliate with the lineage of the wife of her senior owner). Men's prestige was advanced by the acquisition of a concubine, not by the acquisition of an additional wife (1969a:194). Life-cycle feasts are observed on all the Santa Cruz groups, but are perhaps more elaborate here than anywhere else (1969:197). In concluding his paper on the Main Reef Islands, Davenport returns to the theme of individual and society we stressed above. Noting that the social system "could not work if certain trends of individual personality were not present" (1969a:239), he contrasts a social structural explanation (evident in socialization practices that emphasize freedom and ease for young boys) with an indigenous explanation (that leadership qualities are bestowed by supernatural largess) in accounting for the scarcity of young men who demonstrate the competitive spirit necessary to become leaders in "this version of the so-called big-man system" (1969a:240).

In the final paper addressed specifically to Santa Cruz social organization, Davenport presents a description of the northwesterly Outer Reef Islands (Nupani, Matema, Pileni, Nifiloli, Makalobu, Nukapu), focusing especially on the atoll of Nupani and the island of Matema (1972b). Like the Main Reef Islanders, Nupanians were always dependent on trade with the main island of Santa Cruz (here called Deni). Unlike the Main Reef Islanders, however, the Nupanians provided various products of their labor (turtles, turtle shell, smoke-dried shark meat, plaited work) in exchange for currency (1972b:15). Attention to the details of land usage and variations in land tenure associated with different usage strategies provides keys to the understanding of Nupani social organization (1972b:28). The dynamics of Nupani society, which lacks any descent groups or "lineal exogamous categories of any kind" (1972b:29), are to be found in marriage rules and an elaborate etiquette of bride-price payments, contributions to those payments, and the repayment of contributions (1972b:38–39). Here, as elsewhere in Santa Cruz, the men's house association is the core of local political organization (1972b:50–56). It is within the context of the four men's house associations that the political ambitions of the big men get played out. The culture and organization of Matema, at least in the past, were identical to Nupani (1972b:63).

The three islets of Pileni, Nukapu, and Nifiloli share a close historical relationship (demonstrated by their use of the same dialect of Polynesian), and all three differ significantly from Nupani and Matema both in dialect and in recognizing "totemic descent categories" (1972b:72) that were normally exogamous (1972b:85). But, as has been noted in other Polynesian contexts, final control over land resources "is vested not in descent groups, but in corporate residential wards" (1972b:77). Use rights in individual plots are held mostly by individuals. Men's house associations were correlated with these corporate ward groups, providing an important political dynamic (1972b:80). But men's house associations have declined in importance in recent years. All papers in this series indicate the importance of life-cycle rituals.

We have focused attention on the *Baessler-Archiv* series here for two reasons: (1) because these papers are relatively inaccessible to many American anthropologists, and some younger anthropologists may be completely unfamiliar with them, and (2) because they demonstrate Davenport's exceptional ability as an ethnographer and his attention to detail. This was part of the legacy that Bill Davenport attempted to pass along to his students. That our own ethnographic efforts are wanting is in no way to be blamed on him.

In his work on art and aesthetics, Davenport also demonstrates his concern for detail in analysis, while consistently recognizing the importance of understanding material products in their social context. Again, we find the theme of the relation between the individual and society. He notes that in the Eastern Solomon Islands (Star Harbour, Santa Ana, and Santa Catalina), people considered to be especially "talented" possess exceptional skills in many different areas of artistic endeavor. This range of ability is especially important for the various skills needed to make a trading or *bonito* canoe (1987:105; see also 1967b:18). The creative process is attributed to supernatural inspiration (1967b:24; 1987:105). These works of art are both social and individual: "it is an individualized creation and it is a material record of the event for which it was made" (1987:106). This art, moreover, has both aesthetic and ritual value: it is decommoditized. Such objects—whether canoes or ceremonial bowls—may never be thrown away. Nor can they be sold to collectors. When no longer used, they are left to disintegrate (1987:108).

Like the artists of the Eastern Solomon Islands, Bill's special scholarship derives from his range of ability across many different areas. This combination of originality and attention to detail allowed him to write seminal papers on a variety of different topics. His papers on social organization stand as major summaries of classic issues concerning descent and social structure (1959, 1963). The application of game theory to economic transactions (1960) can be seen as an early empirical effort foreshadowing more diffuse approaches which came to be labeled as "processual." Additionally, this paper demonstrates an aspect of Davenport's anthropology which is sometimes overlooked: his interest in formal modeling. His application of formal game theory is intended, among other things, to make manifest and test the kinds of assumptions which underlay ethnographic descriptions. Again, his concern with the relationship of individual and society is evident in his questioning of the, then current, "structure-functionalists' naive assumptions of complete conformity" (1960:10). He returns to economic concerns in the paper "Red Feather Money" (1962). Here his examination of non-Western economics uncovers issues which came to be debated between "formalists" and "substantivists." That it was reprinted both in a general anthropological reader on Melanesia (Langness and Weschler 1971) and in *General Economics* (Anderson et al. 1963) is perhaps sufficient indication of Davenport's success in bringing the two disciplines of anthropology and economics to bear on his analysis.

The paper on red feather money (1962) also recognizes the contradictory definitions of value and the complications that arise when indigenous systems of value come into contact with Western systems of value. This theme is continued in his writing about art twenty-five years later (Davenport 1987) and is consistent with recent anthropological reassessments about collecting and displaying artifacts (see, for example, the papers by Kahn and Welsh in this volume). His longtime recognition that material culture must be understood in its social context foreshadows more recent concerns about what happens when objects are removed from their social context and displayed in museums (1962, 1967b, 1987). In a short article about Tahiti (1969), he deconstructs Western fascination with the exotic many years before it became fashionable to do so.

His papers on sexuality (1977, 1987) are rare efforts to summarize comparative ethnological knowledge about this topic in a systematic and scholarly manner. In providing a very rare and detailed view of sexuality in a non-Western society (1965), he recognized the importance of homosexuality in a Melanesian society some twenty years before it became a popular issue in Melanesian ethnology.

Bill's scholarly influence is reflected in the large number of his papers that were reprinted in different edited volumes and readers

(1959c, 1960a, 1961a, 1962a, 1965, 1967b, 1969b). But for the contributors to this volume and for other students who worked with him, Bill's real contribution is his enthusiasm for anthropology. This enthusiasm was the catalyst which combined his attention to detail, his flexible intellect, and his diverse background with an eclectic range of interests. It made him not only an original scholar but also the most exciting of teachers.

## Overview

This volume originated in a session held at the Annual Meetings of the American Anthropological Association in San Francisco in 1992. Bill's influence, of course, extends well beyond the contributors to this volume. The papers included here are written by students who had him as a teacher and who, as graduate students, worked closely with him in the development of their careers. The papers are diverse in intellectual focus. Most of them are concerned with relatively traditional issues, especially in an unusually consistent focus on kinship. They assume that anthropology is an empirical discipline, still capable of describing some reality which exists outside of the observer. The contributions are based upon intensive fieldwork in "other" cultures. They build their interpretations from detailed description. They examine specific social relationships. The papers are mainly focused on the primary area of Bill's interest, Oceania—including New Guinea, Solomon Islands and Polynesia—although two reflect Bill's interest in Indonesia and Native America. As editors and as anthropologists, however, we remain convinced that one can discern throughout a theme which reflects a respect and enthusiasm for ethnographic knowledge.

We begin in Hawaii, as Bill's anthropological career did. Judy Modell traces the evolution of a research project that, becoming more contextualized, increased in complexity. In her attempts to understand contemporary Hawaiian society, and in particular women's organizations within it, she is forced to come to terms with Hawaiian history as well as the changing expectations and strategies of women.

Laura Zimmer-Tamakoshi is also concerned with changing roles and expectations of women, although in a very different cultural context. Gende women in the Eastern Highlands of Papua New Guinea are altering their own expectations by redeeming their own brideprices, and essentially providing their own daughters with the wherewithal to ensure economically successful marriages.

Working on the northern fringe of the Central Highlands of Papua New Guinea, James Flanagan takes up the theme of individual initiative within constraining systems to look at how men, while attempting to remain equal amongst themselves, continue to attempt to dominate women. Their failure to achieve this dominance enriches rather than impoverishes their cultural experience.

Bill Donner writes from the heart of Davenport's own ethnographic territory: Sikaiana in the Solomon Islands. He is concerned to demonstrate the continued utility of some traditional anthropological notions for the study of a rapidly changing social situation.

Peter Just, too, is concerned with change and modernization. In this instance he focuses on the emergence of new forms of wedding celebration (called *resepsi*) among the Dou Donggo of Sumbawa Island, Indonesia. In a finely woven analysis, Just approaches these innovative gatherings as cultural critiques of both the introduced "Western" notions of appropriate wedding receptions and of traditional cultural practices.

Miriam Kahn's paper places art squarely in its social and ritual context, demonstrating how it becomes radically altered when it is removed. She describes how significant relationships are conveyed through the carving of wooden figurines that guard the aqueduct and protect the vital water supply.

Peter Welsh continues this theme about the context of art but shifts focus to the recontextualization of art as it is displayed in museums. His paper brings us back to the birthplace of anthropology, the museum, and to Bill's concern with museums and museum anthropology. In doing so, however, Welsh is not content to reiterate again the educational value of putting culture on display. Rather, he stresses the tensions and paradoxes inherent in museum presentation, suggesting that in these tensions and paradoxes themselves lie the seeds of a new appreciation of material culture.

With due humility and recognizing their limitations, we offer these papers to Bill Davenport as an extended note of thanks for all he has given to us and to the discipline of anthropology.

## W. H. Davenport Principal Works

1952 "The Religion of Pre-European Hawaii." *Social Process in Hawaii* 16:20–29.
1953 "Marshallese Folklore Types." *Journal of American Folklore* 65:265–66; 66:219–37.
1956 *A Comparative Study of Two Jamaican Fishing Communities.* Ph.D. dissertation, Yale University. Ann Arbor: University Microfilms.
1959a "Comments to R.T. Smith, 'Family Structure and Plantation Systems in the New World'." In *Plantation Systems of the New World*, Social Science Monographs No. 7, pp. 162–63. Washington, D.C.: Pan American Union.
1959b "Marshall Islands Navigational Charts." *Imago Mundi* 14:26–36 (George Beans Award for 1961). (Reprinted in Bobbs-Merrill Reprint Series in Anthropology, No. A-48.)
1959c "Nonunilinear Descent and Descent Groups." *American Anthropologist* 61:557–72. (Reprinted in *Kinship and Family Organization*, ed. B. Farber. Bobbs-Merrill Reprint Series in Anthropology, No. A-49 [New York: Wiley, 1966]; *Readings in Kinship and Social Structure*, ed. N. Graburn, pp. 200–11 [New York: Harper and Row, 1971]; and elsewhere.)
1960a *Jamaican Fishing: A Game Theory Analysis.* Yale University Publications in Anthropology, No. 59. New Haven. (Reprinted in *Peoples and Cultures of the Caribbean*, ed. M. Horowitz. Bobbs-Merrill Reprint Series in Anthropology, No. A-47 [New York: American Museum, 1972].)
1960b "Social Structure." In *Laos, Its People, Its Society, Its Culture*, ed. F.M. LeBar and A. Suddard, pp. 61–76. New Haven: Human Relations Area Files.
1961a "Introduction" and "The Family System of Jamaica." In *Working Papers in Caribbean Social Organization, Social and Economic Studies*, Vol. 10, ed. S.W. Mintz and W. Davenport, pp. 380–85. Jamaica: University College of West Indies Institute of Social and Economic Research. (Reprinted in *A Sourcebook in Marriage, Family and Residence*, ed. P. Bohannan and J. Middleton, pp. 247–84 [New York: American Museum, 1967].)

1961b   "When a Primitive and Civilized Money Meet." In *Proceedings of the 1961 Annual Spring Meeting of the American Ethnological Society*, pp. 64–68. Seattle.

1962a   "Red-feather Money." *Scientific American* 206(3): 94–104. (Reprinted in *General Economics: A Book of Readings*, ed. T.J. Anderson, A.L. Gitlow, and D.E. Diamond, pp. 49–58 [Homewood, Il: R.D. Irwin, 1963]; *Melanesia: Readings on a Culture Area*, ed. L.L. Langness and J.C. Weschler [Scranton: Chandler, 1971].)

1962b   "Comments to A. Capell, 'Oceanic Linguistics Today'." *Current Anthropology* 3:400–2.

1963   "Social Organization." In *Biennial Review of Anthropology*, ed. B.J. Siegel, pp. 178–227. Stanford: Stanford University Press.

1964a   "Hawaiian Feudalism." *Expedition* 6(2): 14–27.

1964b   "Marshall Island Cartography." *Expedition* 6(4): 10–13.

1964c   "Notes on Santa Cruz Voyaging." *Journal of the Polynesian Society* 73:134–42.

1964d   "The Sculpture of La Grande Terre." *Expedition* 7(1): 2–19.

1964e   "Social Structure of Santa Cruz Island." In *Explorations in Cultural Anthropology*, ed. W.H. Goodenough, pp. 57–93. New York: McGraw-Hill.

1965   "Sexual Patterns and Their Regulation in a Society of the Southwest Pacific." In *Sex and Behavior*, ed. F. Beach, pp. 164–207. New York: Wiley. (Reprinted in *An Analysis of Human Sexual Response*, ed. R. and E. Brecher, pp. 175–200 [Boston: Little Brown, 1966].)

1967a   "Melanesian Art and Society." In *Melanesian Art* (Catalogue for an exhibition at University of California, Irvine and Davis), pp. 7–19. University of California.

1967b   "Sculpture from the Eastern Solomon Islands." *Expedition* 10(2): 4–25. (Reprinted in *Art and Aesthetics in Primitive Societies*, ed. C. Jopling, pp. 382–423 [New York: E.P. Dutton, 1971].)

1967c   (with Gülbün Coker) "The Moro Movement of Guadalcanal, British Solomon Islands." *Journal of the Polynesian Society* 76:123–75. (Reprinted as Polynesian Society Reprint No. 13. Wellington, NZ.)

1968a   "Anthropology in the British Solomon Islands." *Expedition* 11(1): 32–34.

1968b   "Social Organization Notes on the Northern Santa Cruz Islands: The Duff Islands (Taumako)." *Baessler-Archiv*, n.f., 16:137–205.

1968c   "Social Organization Notes on the Southern Santa Cruz Islands: Utupua and Vanikoro." *Baessler-Archiv*, n.f., 16:207–75.

1969a   "Social Organization Notes on the Northern Santa Cruz Islands: The Main Reef Islands." *Baessler-Archiv*, n.f., 17:151–243.

1969b   "Some Political and Economic Considerations of the 'Hawaiian Cultural Revolution'." *American Anthropologist* 71:1–19. (Reprinted in Bobbs-Merrill Reprint Series in Anthropology, No. A-408.)

1969c   "Tahiti and the South Sea Legend." *Expedition* 11(4): 12–15.

1970   "Two Social Movements in the British Solomons that Failed and Their Political Consequences." In *The Politics of Melanesia*, ed. M.W. Ward, pp. 162–72. Canberra: Australian National University.

1972a   "Preliminary Archaeological Excavations in the Eastern Solomon Islands." *Archaeology and Physical Anthropology in Oceania* 7:165–83.

1972b   "Social Organization Notes on the Northern Santa Cruz Islands: The Outer Reef Islands." *Baessler-Archiv*, n.f., 20:11–95.

1974   (and J. Halley Cox) *Hawaiian Sculpture*. Honolulu: The University Press of Hawaii.

1975a   "A Population of the Outer Reef Islands, British Solomon Islands Protectorate." In *Pacific Atoll Populations*, ed. V. Carroll, pp. 64–116. Association of Social Anthropology. Oceania Monograph Series, No. 3. Honolulu: The University Press of Hawaii.

1975b   "Lyric Verse and Ritual in the Santa Cruz Islands." *Expedition* 18(1): 39–47.

1977   "Sex in Cross-Cultural Perspective." In *Human Sexuality in Four Perspectives*, ed. F. Beach, pp. 115–63. Baltimore: Johns Hopkins University Press.

1979   "Marriage in Cross-Cultural Perspective." In *The Childhood Emotional Pattern in Marriage*, ed. L.J. Saul, pp. 68–99. Philadelphia: Lippincott.

1981a   "Male Initiation in Aoriki." *Expedition* 23(2): 4–19.

1981b "The National Gallery Presents 'The Art of the Pacific Islands'." *Studies in Anthropology and Visual Communications* 7(1): 74–81.

1985a "The Thailand Controversy in Retrospect." In *Social Contexts of American Ethnology, 1840–1984*, ed. J. Helm, pp. 65–72. The 1984 Proceedings of the American Ethnological Society. Washington, D.C.

1985b *A Miniature Figure from Santa Cruz Island*. Bulletin No. 28 of the Musée Barbier-Muller, Geneva.

1986 "Two Kinds of Value in the Eastern Solomon Islands." In *The Social Life of Things*, ed. A. Appadurai, pp. 95–109. New York: Cambridge University Press.

1987 "An Anthropological Approach." In *Paradigms of Sexual Behavior*, ed. W. Geer, pp. 197–236. New York: Plenum Press.

1988a "Introduction" and "Selections from the Exhibition." *Expedition* (Special Issue: Borneo, ed. William Davenport) 30(1).

1988b "George Peter Murdock's Classification of 'Consanguineal Kin Groups'." *Behavior Science Research* 22:10–22.

1988c "Preface" and "Additions to the Catalog." In *Hawaiian Sculpture* by J.H. Cox and W.H. Davenport. Rev. ed. Honolulu: University of Hawaii Press.

1989 "Taemfaet: Experiences and Reactions of Santa Cruz Islanders during the Battle for Guadalcanal." In *The Pacific Theater: Island Representations of World War II*, ed. G.M. White and L. Lindstrom, pp. 257–78. Pacific Island Monograph Series, No. 8. Honolulu: University of Hawaii Press.

1990a "The Canoes of Santa Ana and Santa Catalina Islands." In *Art as a Means of Communication in Pre-Literate Societies: The Proceedings of the Wright International Symposium on Primitive and Pre-Columbian Art, Jerusalem, 1985*, ed. D. Eban, pp. 97–125. Jerusalem: The Israel Museum.

1990b "The Figurative Sculpture of Santa Cruz Island." In *Art and Identity in Oceania*, ed. F. Alan and Louise Hanson, pp. 98–110. Honolulu: University of Hawaii Press, Honolulu.

1991 "The Santa Cruz Islanders." In *Encyclopedia of World Cultures*. Vol. 2, *Oceania*, pp. 290–92. Boston: G.K. Hall.

1992 "Adult-Child Sexual Relations in Cross-Cultural Perspective."

In *The Sexual Abuse of Children: Theory, Research and Therapy*, Vol. I, ed. James Geer and William O'Donohue, pp. 73–80. Hillsdale, N.J.: Lawrence Erlbaum Associates.

1994 *Piʻo: An Enquiry into the Marriage of Brothers and Sisters and Other Close Relatives in Old Hawaiʻi.* University of Pennsylvania Publications in Anthropology No. 5. Lanham, Md.: University Press of America.

1996a "Wogosia: An Annual Renewal Rite in the Eastern Solomon Islands." *Expedition* 38(3): 24–40.

1996b Pacific Islands 6. Sculpture." In *The Dictionary of Art*, Vol. 23, pp. 730–33. New York: Groves Dictionary.

1996c "Santa Cruz Islands." In *The Dictionary of Art*, Vol. 27, pp. 778–79. New York: Groves Dictionary.

1996d "Money." In *The Encyclopedia of Cultural Anthropology.* Vol. 3, *M–R*, pp. 805–08. New York: Henry Holt.

n.d. "Marshall Islands Stick Charts." In *Encyclopedia of the History of Science, Technology and Medicine in Non-Western Cultures.* Garland Publishing Company. Forthcoming.

n.d. "New Data on the Early Iron Industry of the Sarawak River Region." *Sarawak Museum Journal.* Forthcoming.

n.d. "Strophics and Society in Santa Cruz Islands." *Garland Encyclopedia of World Music.* Washington, D.C.: Garland Publishing. Forthcoming.

## Museum Exhibitions

1964 The Sculpture of La Grande Terre. The University Museum, University of Pennsylvania

1965–70 Pacific Islands Cultures. The University Museum, University of Pennsylvania

1967 Sculpture from the Eastern Solomon Islands. The University Museum, University of Pennsylvania

1967 Melanesian Art. University of California, Irvine

1968–72 Austronesia: The Cultures of Indonesia, New Guinea, and Australia. The University Museum, University of Pennsylvania

1969 Art of New Guinea. Adlai E. Stevenson College, University of California, Santa Cruz

1969 (with David Crownover and Bengt Danielsson) Gauguin

and the South Seas. The University Museum, University of Pennsylvania
1983– Polynesia. The University Museum, University of Pennsylvania
1989–90 The Dayaks: Peoples of the Borneo Rainforest. The University Museum, University of Pennsylvania

# Missionary Ventures in Hawaii: 19th Century Wives, 20th Century Social Workers

*Judith Modell*

## Introduction

Years ago, when Bill Davenport first introduced me to the term *hapa-haole* (part *haole* or part white), I never imaged it would play a role in my life or that I would end up doing fieldwork in Hawaii. He brought the term up in the context of a reading course that concentrated on Pacific ethnography, for Bill used literature from the Pacific to expand my anthropological training. We talked about "culture and personality," about language and symbolism, about gender roles, about ritual and social organization. Always Bill's sparkling imagination took off from data; he impressed me with the brilliance of his insights and the theoretical leaps he could make, and he impressed me with the need to ground all this in "evidence"—the stuff that was out there, visible and tangible. I have tried to bring his lesson about theory and data into my work. But I never thought I would apply that lesson in Hawaii or end up recalling those conversations in detail as I sifted through the material I began to gather one summer in Honolulu.

There was another lesson in those conversations with Bill, one I am not sure I will ever be able to learn as well as he taught it. That was a lesson of compassion, a quality I also find in his writings, from those on sex to those on sculpture. A tone pervades his writings, as it did his talk, that suggests sympathy for the hardships human beings suffer and humility before the diversity of solutions individuals bring to the inevitable crises of life—whether in Jamaica, or in New Haven, or in the "paradise of the Pacific." This reflects not an easy sentimentality, but a respectful recognition of human dignity. Moreover, attention to the person—or, perhaps, the human condition—intertwines with a fine sense of the complexity of culture and of social organization. Bill never told a simple story, not even when he told anecdotes about his own years in Hawaii.

I would like to capture both the compassion and the complexity in my writings on Hawaii—a project that has already accumulated a number of strands, approaches, and arguments. I will briefly summarize my research and then introduce the subject that forms the body of this paper.

My project began as a study of adoption among Hawaiians in the state of Hawaii. Specifically, I intended to examine the continuities and the changes in "customary" forms of adoption as Hawaiians became part of an American state and a "modern" world. Given this interest, my research site was, and still is, Honolulu and surrounding communities. What happens, I initially asked, to the famous frequent and casual passing around of children in the presence of an American legal and child welfare system?[1] But as I pursued my fieldwork, I realized my subject was more complicated; adoption could not be treated apart from other forms of child placement and from the circumstances in which 20th century urban Hawaiians found themselves. I discovered, in other words, that adoption is only one aspect of a pervasive interaction between Hawaiian families and American state institutions.

The interaction, moreover, involves not only a clash of behaviors but also a confrontation between differing cultural ideologies of family, kinship, and parenthood. After several field trips, I realized that none of these matters concerning children, parents, and families could be separated from the politics of sovereignty in Hawaii.[2] These politics have changed markedly over the past decade and contemporary arguments for a "Hawaiian nation" pull in their wake programs and policies relating to the domestic arena. Demands for cultural autonomy affected virtually every Hawaiian person I met. And for those who would never sit in front of a bulldozer or call for Hawaiian independence, asserting cultural autonomy meant protecting the integrity of an "affective" domain.[3]

The subject I focus on in this chapter is related to and expands my original interest in the interaction between Hawaiian families and an American legal and social system. I compare late 20th century social work endeavors with early 19th century missionization efforts—and social workers with mission wives. A comparative discussion of these do-gooder movements reveals a persistent interest in "converting" the Hawaiian, modified by markedly different styles of achieving that conversion. It also reveals the persistent connection between "saving" an individual and "redeeming" a nation. The conviction that transforming individuals can rescue a people, I argue, organizes 20th century social work activities as urgently as it did 19th century missionary activities. Like their forebears, social workers link the character of the client to changes in the state of the land.

Like their forebears, too, social workers turned to the domestic arena and specifically to the women presumed to be central in that arena. The 19th century goal was to create "good wives and mothers" in order to shore up a degenerate society; the 20th century version holds that teaching women a sense of responsibility can counteract the perceived disorder in a Hawaiian community.[4] For missionary wives, this meant teaching Hawaiian *wahine* how to be proper homemakers and helpmeets. For social workers, this means empowering women so they can be "agents" in their own lives. Yet the impulse—the goal of conversion—is not much different. Thus, observed responses of contemporary women can shed light on the probable responses of 19th century women to the reformulation of identity that conversion entails. Exploring those responses constitutes my concluding section.

The process of conversion involves both content and form, principle and practice. As I use the concept, form refers not only to means but also to aesthetic and sensual elements; I am talking about a *style* of interaction. The word *style* is particularly apt, befitting a context where one often hears "Hawaiian-style" or "*haole*-style" used to characterize patterns of behavior.[5] Style, as used in the following pages, includes gestures and mannerisms, expressions of intimacy and of intimidation—the texture of an encounter between individuals that necessarily occurs on a non-verbal as well as a verbal plane.

This aspect of the relationship between "visitor" and "native" has not been given much attention, and my analysis of style in the Hawaiian instance will, I hope, provide new insights into an old story.

Such an analysis exposes the multistranded nature of conversion and of the responses to being converted. Recognizing this in turn allows me to uncover modes of resistance on the part of "clients"—the Hawaiian women who found themselves (or chose to be) subjects of the good-hearted ministrations offered by missionary wives and by social workers.[6] How those who "benefited" reacted to those who "granted benefits" is not a major theme in the literature on missionaries and on contemporary social workers. Donors and their assessments tend to determine calculations of success or failure; the client is denied a voice and only her situation is represented.[7] Using data from two three-month periods of participation in women's groups on Oahu, I construct a countervailing interpretation based on the reactions of those who generously accepted the efforts of "good-hearted" visitors.

In 1989, I participated in several different women's groups and in 1990 I became a regular member of one group. Sponsored by a downtown Honolulu agency, the group met once a week in a town on the Waianae Coast. The population it served was one in which family breakdown, alcohol and drug use, and domestic violence were prevalent (State of Hawaii 1990a, 1990b). Women came for various reasons, and reacted variously to what went on each week. As I became accepted, less *haole* than female, participants drew me into their confidence, adding personal comments to the responses and behavior I observed at meetings—and at other times, for these women hung around together when there were no meetings. These diverse expressions demonstrated an alternation between acceptance and rejection of the group's goals that I view as a mode of resistance. I extend this interpretation to posit a similar resistance on the part of 19th century *wahine* to 19th century missionaries.

A few caveats. Recently, studies of missionaries and mission movements have become a significant part of anthropological and historical literature.[8] My interest lies less in the details of missionary policy and impact such literature describes than in the broader principles and dilemmas raised by missionary ventures in general.[9] In the pages that follow, then, the differences between types of missionaries—by religion, background, or administrative organization—are less salient than a common purpose captured in the phrase "regenerating a nation through its wives and mothers" (see Grimshaw 1989b:26). I pay somewhat more attention to the differences among 20th century social workers, partly because the people I met in Hawaii noted these differences and partly because I observed them myself. But in this, as in the historical instance, my primary aim is to examine the ramifying impact of a principle that holds a people can be saved through the transformation of its women.

I must also explain my usage of "Hawaiian," a term both problematic and politicized. In this paper, "Hawaiian" refers to people of Hawaiian ancestry, including those who identify themselves as Hawaiian and those who are designated Hawaiian by private and public agencies (e.g., the Department of Health). A majority of women in the Waianae Coast women's group were Hawaiian by this definition; others who play a role in my paper lived in Hawaiian Homelands areas and tended to assert their Hawaiian way of life.[10] For missionary women, of course, all "clients" were Hawaiian.

I begin with an account of my participation in the women's group, then use data from fieldwork to re-examine material on missionary interventions. My emphasis on the domestic side of these ventures follows a line of argument taken in the important work *Family and Gender in the Pacific* (Jolly and Macintyre 1989). Here, Jolly and Macintyre argue that family and household policies were crucial to the impact of missionaries on Pacific Island societies. The story of mothers and children, in other words, is not trivial or digressive but central to understanding a vast historical movement. I am also influenced by the point made by Sahlins and Kirch in their recent *Anahulu: The Anthropology of History* (1992), where they show the significance of very particular actions, motives, and greeds to the long story that is history. Although they are not alone in privileging the "small," theirs is a particularly cogent example of micro-ethnography and the dent such an approach makes in the Western hegemonic discourse on colonialism (Linnekin 1990; Sahlins 1985). And so I turn to a local group, its meetings attended by between 6 and 12 people on any one day. At meetings, the script of global change is writ small, forcefully, and consequentially.

## "The Duties of the Mother"

The group I attended was in some ways typical of new social work strategies in Hawaii, and in some ways unique. Like other women's groups, it drew on notions of self-help and awareness that were rooted in the consciousness-raising emphases of a post-1960s American culture. The Waianae group also reflected the policies of its parent agency, one that in embracing modern principles of social work took on an American tone.[11] What actually occurred at meetings, however, depended on the particular facilitators who happened to be working on the Waianae Coast. And though all were supposed to follow the dictates of the agency, each did so with her or his own agenda, goals, and style.

Kathy and Tina ran the group I joined in 1990. Like most social workers in the agency, they were not Hawaiian by ancestry or culture; they were, however, *local*—born and raised in the islands—and they made an effort to present that side of themselves to the women.[12] The participants were mainly Hawaiian or part-Hawaiian, not surprisingly, since the group met in an Hawaiian area and Hawaiian families tended to show the signs of collapse that elicit agency involvement.

The women came for different reasons—and not always every week (attendance was no more regular here than it was at any other "official" gathering). A few had been advised to attend by a social worker, and one or two were told that this was the only way they could regain custody of children who were in foster care. Others came because they were suffering from abuse and humiliation at home, and still others because they had heard the group was "a good way" to handle problems with men, sex, and children—in that order of priority. The first meeting I went to was especially well-attended, partly, I realized, because the man who ran a neighborhood men's group was going to be there. In retrospect, that meeting provided important clues for interpreting subsequent meetings and for comparing modern with early mission ventures.

The morning's meeting was held in a small clapboard house behind a large community center. (It started almost an hour late, a thrift shop in the basement of the center proving irresistible.) The meeting opened, as all would, with the facilitators asking the women to summarize the past week and their feelings about it. This was followed by a relaxed, unstructured discussion of what had been said and then by the day's business. David was the day's business and his arrival called attention to the subject that dominated every meeting of the women's group: relationships with men. The task of transforming these Hawaiian women, I saw, would revolve around that dimension of their lives.

David brought lessons from his work with the men's group and directed them toward the women.[13] Referring to episodes in his own life as well as to the conversations in his group, David portrayed men as vulnerable, insecure, and "culturally" violent; he never suggested abusive behavior was natural, but he did suggest it was cultural and situational. He drew the women along with him, persuading them to sympathize with men's issues while convincing them they could "handle" these issues. He managed at once to assert "maleness" and to impress upon the women the significance of their own behaviors in a relationship.

A modern statement about care and respect for other people's needs, David's message also reflected Hawaiian cultural values in its emphasis on sex, sensuality, and pleasure.[14] Moreover, his own manner and gestures reiterated these values; flirtatious and provocative, his was not the presentation of a puritanical missionary or of a conventional *haole* social worker. But it was, I later understood, the message of someone whose intention as much as any missionary or conventional social worker was to convert the people he instructed.

At subsequent meetings, Kathy and Tina followed David's example in conjoining sex and self-confidence, pleasure and empowerment. David's appearance had only galvanized a subject that was never missing from anyone's conversation. Whatever the events of their week, the women invariably sprinkled their summaries with titillating references to their own and their boyfriends' sexual desires. In relishing details, they may have been testing my *haole* responses; more likely they were testing the limits of Kathy's and Tina's professional demeanor. But Kathy and Tina were not to be baited; they listened and laughed and let the stories unwind. At the end of the introductory period, they might point to one or another person's progress, but I never heard them criticize or condemn anyone's reported behavior. The next phase of the meeting usually involved conversations in a talk-story mode—each person meandering through anecdotes, with little direction from the facilitators.[15]

Yet, listening hard and weekly, I noted that themes did emerge and a model of womanhood seemed to take shape under Tina's and Kathy's invisible guidance. The contours of the model were familiar to me: taking responsibility for oneself and one's actions. The model, however, was neither rigorously drawn nor imposed upon the group. Kathy and Tina did not simply "transplant" *haole* womanhood to the Waianae Coast; rather, they planted seeds of change which would result in a "new" woman at the end of the sessions.[16] Moreover, this new woman would not be the "dutiful wife and mother" of an earlier missionary venture, but the empowered woman of modern times. The model—as Kathy's and Tina's laughter at the pervasive sexual innuendoes showed—left room for the elements of Hawaiian womanhood a century of missionization and Americanization could not erase. For Kathy and Tina had inherited an interaction whose roots lay in the first migration of "do-gooding" women to the "native communities" of the Sandwich Islands.

Missionary wives came to Hawaii in the early 19th century in the company of their husbands.[17] They came to convert and to civilize, to turn the heathen into Christian and the savage into citizen. Not at the time called missionaries themselves, these wives were expected to act in the domestic arena, seeing to family matters while their husbands handled public matters without, it was hoped, becoming politicians. Members of the Sandwich Islands mission "agreed that they ought not to interfere in political or secular matters *except* where issues of religion and sound morals were involved." This disclaimer, as the writer points out, left "considerable running room" (Hutchinson 1987:72–73). Exactly what ought to be accomplished—the wives with the mothers and children, the missionaries with the men—was decided by individuals whose position, locations, and times of arrival influenced their actions.

The American missionaries did share a staunch Puritanical perspective. The clearest part of their agenda came out of the somber religion they practiced at home, as they tried to turn Hawaiian women and men into good daughters and sons of New England (Hutchinson 1987:43; Grimshaw 1989a:155). In one respect, the task seemed formidable; missionary wives perceived anything but domesticity in the Hawaiian *wahine* who lolled (or so it seemed) around the edges of mission compounds. In another respect, however, missionary wives found their task all too easy; generous and cooperative, Hawaiian women listened to the Christian message with as much pleasure as they greeted the sailors and the goods carried on American ships. Moreover, when Queen Kaahumanu became a convert and commoner women followed her lead, triumph seemed in sight.[18]

From the 1820s on, the mission wives concentrated on molding a dutiful wife and mother out of the *wahine* who from the missionary perspective seemed to like nothing better than their own pleasures. The very proof of their heathen nature, in fact, lay in their blatant disregard of hearth and household. Wherever the missionary wives looked, they saw evidence of familial disorder. Not only did Hawaiian women give themselves to sailors, traders, and merchants, but they also showed no sense of loyalty to a partner. Worst of all, perhaps, Hawaiian women seemed to let their children run wild; wandering from place to place, Hawaiian children often ended up in the mission house. And while some mission wives took upon themselves the task of educating Hawaiian children, others simply saw this as an inconvenience and, even more significantly, as an indication of how much work they had to do to transform Hawaiian women into proper Christian souls.[19]

And so they set about their tasks, eventually forming an association that had elements in common with a 20th century women's group. In 1834, the mission wives created the Sandwich Islands' Maternal Association, initially to comfort and help one another. "The primary object," explained Mercy Whitney, "was to throw light on the path of duty before us. It will also improve our minds, and qualify us for the better discharge of the duties of our station" (Grimshaw 1989a:115). As Whitney suggests, talk among the wives was directed toward betterment of the mission; reassured by one another, they turned back clear-eyed to the task of conversion. Out of the diffuse exchanges at the Maternal Association meetings came the model of womanhood that ought, if the mission succeeded, regenerate the lives of Hawaiian people.

The first task was to create a mother out of these apparently free-spirited Hawaiian women—a task Tina and Kathy did not include in their agenda. By contrast, the missionary program evinced a strong faith in the powers of motherhood. "In our opinion," stated the Lahaina mission report in 1833, "all that ever has been written on the subject of a mother's influence, has come far short of giving it the high rank which it really holds. Could the influence of a pious mother be brought to bear upon the children of Hawaii, then these islands might be transformed" (Grimshaw 1989b:37).

A more realistic mission wife might have concluded that Hawaiian women should be, if not pious, at least skilled in the ways of running a household; careful management, American women knew, kept a woman tied to her hearth, her husband, and her children. On October 6, 1841, the Maternal Association recorded its motivating ideology: "The duties of the mother begin in the morning; they end not with the day.... Others may have respite. Others may for a time throw of [sic] care, and anxiety and responsibility. But the mother never can do so" (Hawaiian Mission Children's Society *mss*). The endless care of family was to be the Hawaiian woman's lot.

"The meaning of marriage and chaste sexuality would be made plain; the role of housewife and mother would be elucidated; then the influence of the Hawaiian woman, at the center of her well-regulated family, would ripple outward, redeeming wayward children, errant husbands, and finally, the whole kingdom for godly living" (Grimshaw 1989a:161). Those sentences evoked the best of all possible worlds; failing the redemption of the kingdom, the missionary wives could find satisfaction in transforming Hawaiian women from sexual "sirens" into maternal helpmeets. What this amounted to, as the women in the Waianae group would put it, was a *haole*-fication of the Hawaiian *wahine*.

"Hawaiian women were presented with the model of American femininity, the full force of the American's material wealth, skills and the missionaries' undeniable altruism and forceful personal attributes" (Grimshaw 1989b:26). Ultimately, missionary wives hoped, Christianity would flower upon this model of womanhood. In the interim, they turned their attention to practical activities, teaching manners and housekeeping skills. Too, missionary wives began to suspect that church attendance might be an unreliable measure of progress toward piety; convincing women to stay home was more worthwhile than encouraging them to come out every Sunday morning.

Domestic training supplanted religious training, though the two were not mutually exclusive. "The foremost goal of the American mission women was to convert Hawaiian women to a genuine piety, the mainspring as they saw it of all worthy moral behavior" (Grimshaw 1989b:26). The route to such conversion, by mid-century, sounded like a mainland finishing school: reading, writing, sewing, and cooking. "The role of the wife," mission wives were told, "is to maintain the house and all that is within" (Grimshaw 1989b:35).

It was a powerful picture of female character and one that persisted into the 20th century. The links between domesticating women, civilizing individuals, and saving the nation did not collapse under territorial and then state governance; custom and legal code preserved the nexus. Kathy and Tina inherited this tradition, modifying it with post-1960s feminism and their own absorption in local culture. Yet there is an echo: rescuing women and giving them a sense of power did bear upon the state of the "people." And though Kathy and Tina would have roundly rejected the language of a mission manual, their own remarks ultimately followed the same path from a "good woman" through a strong family to a "redeemed nation." The difference, and it is an important one, lay in the *style* of presentation: the model was offered, but not from above or inscribed in stone.

A good part of the content of the Waianae Coast women's group meetings, then, echoed an earlier century. Shoring up domestic life, giving women a sense of their own identities and abilities to act in the world, providing an example of "good" character pervaded the women's group as strongly as it did the Maternal Association of the Sandwich Islands mission. But, as I have suggested, the style of each venture differed; the differences allow me to penetrate the nature of Hawaiian resistance to missionization in both periods.

## David's Visit Re-Visited

Thinking about David's visit that first time also provides a starting point for my discussion of style—the patterns of interaction that filled out the encounter between *haole* and Hawaiian.

I mentioned David's arrival, but not the spirited greetings he exchanged with the women. A sexual shiver spread through the room when he came in; the women joked about the *aloha* kissing, comparing David's performance as he moved from one person to the next.[20] David encouraged this response and so did Kathy and Tina, who joined in the teasing along with everyone else. With David as focus, Kathy and Tina established a firm identification with the women in the group; they would play with this identification in subsequent meetings. But the terms were set: a shared sexuality would be the basis for creating a shared sensibility.

This style of conversion represented a self-conscious decision on the part of the two facilitators, as well as being a mode they knew from having grown up in island culture. That this *was* a decision became clear when I met Sylvia, a facilitator of another Waianae Coast women's group sponsored by the same downtown agency. Sylvia's style was more directive than either Tina's or Kathy's; when they were being kind, they called her "too motherly" but they meant too bossy. They disliked the way she intervened in the women's stories and, by implication, in their lives. From Kathy's and Tina's point of view, Sylvia acted superior to the women—a stance Kathy and Tina bent over backwards to avoid.[21] Sitting on the floor, laughing and joking with the women, Tina and Kathy formed an even more striking contrast with their predecessors than with their fellow social workers. Their demeanor would have astonished the stiff and proper Mercy Whitneys of an earlier era.

Missionary wives shunned the identification Tina and Kathy worked to maintain, struggling instead to preserve the distance that justified their errand in the wilderness. Yet the distancing was not unproblematic; one worried entry in the journal of the Maternal Association, for instance, reveals a doubt about the method. On June 5, 1840, the Maternal Association set itself a topic of discussion: "What bearing has this principle of nonintercourse upon our duties to the heathen?" (Hawaiian Children's Mission Society *mss*). Twenty years into the mission, the women realized how large a gap had opened between themselves and the native women. They had to ask whether that distance also diminished their success in converting the heathen to the *haole* model of womanhood. They were expected to set an example of duty and docility. How effective could an example be if there were no intercourse between the two groups?

A manual of instructions distributed to the Sandwich Islands mission filled in the details of the example wives were to be. In 1838 the Prudential Committee of the American Board of Commissioners for Foreign Missions reminded its workers that wives have a duty "to show to the rude and depraved islanders an effective example of the purity, and dignity, and loveliness, the salutary and vivifying influence, the attractive and celestial excellence, which christianity can impart to the female character" (Hawaiian Children's Mission Society *mss*). Not only was this a burden that any hardworking, often discouraged American missionary woman might find hard to bear, but the phrasing itself also exacerbated the sense of difference that was never far beneath the surface of interactions with native women. To be told at once of the "rude and depraved" state of their subjects and of the "celestial excellence" of their own nature did not bode well for an easy intercourse between *haole* and native women.[22]

Eventually it was less by example than by precept that missionary women attempted to convert the heathen. Unable always to represent "purity" to the "depraved," mission wives turned their attention to teaching native women how to read, how to cook, and how to sew— lessons that did not depend upon intimate interaction or identification with the native women. They found Hawaiian women to be willing pupils, and hoped that "purity, and, dignity, and loveliness" would follow in the wake of practical lessons. In case anyone forgot, a 1844 manual reiterated the goal: "The role of the wife is to maintain the house and all that is within. It is her responsibility to look after the husband's clothing and the food—the household chores—setting in place the sleeping quarters and all else that is within" (quoted in Grimshaw 1989b:35).

The shift from evangelization to social amelioration meant a move from intimacy to instruction as the mode of conversion.[23] By the 1840s, missionary wives were less "sisters" than teachers of the native women. As if to mark the change, fewer wives learned Hawaiian, while deciding that American children should not talk "Hawaiian-style" either. On June 2, 1840, an extra long entry in the Records of the Maternal Association worried over "child intercourse with natives," leading to a further separation of *haole* from Hawaiian.[24] By mid-century, mission wives insisted upon their differences from Hawaiian women and renegotiated the meaning of "uplifting the heathen." This turn to the practical and the pedagogic, however, left them without a sure measure of success: was the end of their efforts to be the creation of a seamstress and cook, even one who stayed home with her husband and children?[25]

A century later Tina and Kathy faced analogous problems in calculating the success of their efforts. With a style that contrasted in its intimacy and identification with that of missionary wives, Kathy and Tina still expected to transform the characters of the women who attended Friday morning meetings. And they had to establish signs of transformation, an indication that the goal had been reached. One way they did this sounded an echo to mission-style approaches: they conveyed an image of their own accomplishments and of the order in their lives.

But this was subtle, and specific methods of conversion were never an outstanding part of group meetings. Kathy and Tina did not teach or preach; nor did they show films, as David did, to direct the consciousness-raising. The one morning Kathy did modify her style reminded me that in fact the two facilitators had all along been persuading the women to change—to alter their "life-styles" and to reconsider their characteristic patterns of behavior. On that morning, after the initial exchange of stories, Kathy asked us to make collages. Magazines were available so we could cut out pictures of what we wanted our lives to be like, how we "really" wanted to be as women, what our fondest wishes were. When we finished, we searched for common themes; these included the importance of education, of being able to manage a household, and of treating children gently and respectfully. But, as evoked by the pictures of elegant models on almost every collage, being stunning and independent struck everyone's fancy. The women chuckled about this, and about how they could be "on their own" and still have "all the sex" they wanted. Kathy and Tina encouraged the genie out of the bottle, letting the image of powerful female sensuality instantiate more abstract elements of self-transformation. The collage constituted the most deliberate lesson in conversion I ever saw Kathy or Tina teach.

I observed a similar technique used in another group on the Waianae Coast. In 1989, I attended meetings for mothers held by a group called Time-Out Nursery. Established to give mothers "respite" from their children, the group combined mission-style instruction with 20th century style consciousness-raising.[26] At one meeting, a native-Hawaiian activist worked with the six women who had come. Kawena asked us to represent in pictures the kind of women we wanted to be and the kind of world we wanted to live in. Like the collage, this exercise encouraged the women to explore their own ideals and wishes; afterwards, under Kawena's low-keyed direction, we constructed an image of the "good" woman—one which transcended cultural differences.

Like Kathy and Tina, Kawena granted the women authority over their own lives. She did not take a privileged position or tell us how to interpret our drawings; rather, she emphasized the kind of free conversation that resembled both Hawaiian talk-story and American consciousness-raising. By the end, there were no "outsiders" in the group, not even me—who in looks and language was unmistakably *haole*. There was a model of womanhood, and with it a strong sense of the direction "we" ought to take in our lives. If not Christian conversion, the goal here was certainly change.

Mission-style intervention has by no means disappeared from Hawaii or from the Waianae Coast. The persistence of that style of conversion was apparent, for instance, in parent-training workshops run by The Institute for Family Enrichment (TIFE). The workshops concentrate on improving family relationships with an eye toward increasing the control Hawaiians (and others) have over the circumstances of their lives. One afternoon I attended a workshop held for the residents of a local housing project; about half the residents were Hawaiian. That day two mothers came, their children in tow. The tone at the meeting was strikingly different from either the women's group or Time-Out. Principles were articulated, portions of books read out loud, and hypothetical crises created in order to elicit responses. The instructors did more talking than the participants, offering advice and familiar wisdom: "when a child is behaving badly, distract her with another toy or activity." I felt as if I were in a classroom, and a *haole* classroom at that.[27]

TIFE was by no means insensitive to the diversity of cultures on Oahu or to the particular stringencies attached to being Hawaiian in an American state in the 1990s. In manner of presentation, however, the workshops resembled the Maternal Association, with a reliance on a universal standard of proper behavior and a conviction that some people needed guidance from others. Following these principles, the group leaders took on an air of distance from the participants. Yet on the continuum of agencies dealing with Hawaiian people, TIFE was closer to the women's group than to the agency almost everyone I met considered the worst example of *haole* proselytizing, Child Protective Services (CPS).

CPS had absolute standards for parental or, effectively, maternal behavior, and social workers often acted on perceived failures with precipitate speed.[28] It might well appear, to the parent who thus "lost" a child, that her child was being removed because her family did not look *haole*. And while it is true that CPS workers acted on the principles established by an American state and an American judiciary, even more troubling to the people I met was the sense that intervention had been unilateral: an unnegotiated assessment of parent-child interactions. From this point of view, a standard had been imposed without any elicitation of people's own understandings of the situation—the worst outcome of a do-gooding venture.

My aim is not to criticize CPS, whose overextended workers faced one emergency after another, so much as to suggest the multistranded nature of Hawaiian responses to missionizing endeavors. People who had experience with CPS practices understood these as representing a model of parental behavior that was "foreign" and CPS decisions as imposing an ideal of family broadscale. Significantly, too, the model came clothed in a style that was distant, bureaucratic, non-intimate and non-empathetic. Hawaiian interpretations of 20th century mission ventures might well be represented by the contrast between Tina, in her lavishly colored sarongs, and a CPS worker in her blue suit, answering a call from a school principal and taking a child to the local police station.[29]

These styles, as much as the content of an action, constituted the "other" against which Hawaiian people developed a pattern of resistance. The effort to transform an individual and improve her life characterized all the endeavors I have described—from the Maternal Association through the women's group on the Waianae Coast—but the methods differed; nuances of gesture, touch, and conversation provided the palette with which Hawaiians developed strategic responses and drove a wedge into the system. The inscription of a distinct *style* on behaviors increased the intricacy of the interaction between "clients," or "heathen," and do-gooders, while also allowing the kind of resistance I describe in the next section: subtle, sexual, and self-conscious.

Before exploring the issue of resistance, let me summarize my argument so far. From the 19th through the 20th century, Hawaiian women learned similar lessons from the people whose concern was their welfare. But they learned these lessons in different formats and, effectively, in different languages. Like the group participants, Tina and Kathy spoke a lilting pidgin; mission wives, by contrast, set their clipped New England accents against the "talk" they heard in the field. Styles of being expert, too, varied, ranging from Kawena's autobiographical reflections to the stiff instructions given at a TIFE meeting. Styles of physical interaction probably differed most of all; mission wives would not have been comfortable with the kissing, hugging, and ribald teasing that was central to Waianae Coast women's group meetings. Such validation of sensuality and sexuality modified the *haole* model of womanhood promulgated by the American agency Kathy and Tina represented. Such validation gave Hawaiian women the methods for resisting which I now describe.

## Sandy's Shower

By the 1840s, missionary wives doubted whether the model of Christian womanhood they taught had taken hold. "All Hawaiian women," they despairingly concluded, "fell far short of the desired model of true womanhood that they had tried so hard to impose." Good puritans, some blamed themselves: "'What in me hinders their salvation?' Lucia Smith plaintively asked her friend Juliette Cooke, as she watched women drift away from her instruction" (Grimshaw 1989b:40). Others must have decided the clay was unmoldable after all, only deceptively pliable. How Hawaiian women viewed their New England lessons has not been as well documented—and the statements they did make seemed to arouse suspicion in those who heard them. "The expression of the lips merely, is no sure indication of the heart," complained a missionary wife five years before Lucia Smith's plaintive cry (Grimshaw 1989b:39). No one could tell how long "good actions" would last when the mission wife was not there to supervise.

The women I met on the Waianae Coast claimed they benefited from the women's group, appreciated Time-Out, and saw the value in a program like TIFE's. The social workers might well have been pleased with their "conversion." Yet there were limits to the Hawaiian women's acceptance, which I saw and heard. These observations form the basis for my conclusion that no mission venture is unresisted and that Hawaiian *wahine* know exactly what they are doing in that regard. If such resistance has not yet been noted, it is because scholars have not looked in the right places.

I went to the women's group regularly for three months and meetings, if not consistently attended, were always talkative and lively. Glancing around the room, I certainly would have said the women enjoyed the group; exactly what they learned was not so obvious. The women discussed this themselves, evaluating the advantages of going. On one level, as they all admitted, it was simply a pleasure to sit around and talk without interruption for two hours. On another level, which they also appreciated, the participants learned they were not alone in their experiences. But like the missionary wives, Tina and Kathy expected more, as did the agency for which they worked. They expected a transformation in character, a conversion from one model of womanhood to another so that an individual was no longer at risk of being abused or of neglecting her children.

As I came to know the women in the group better, I realized they drew definite lines around how converted they would be. At the shower for Sandy, just before the last meeting, these lines appeared, drawn vividly in the midst of the eating, gossip, and general hilarity of such events. Sandy had joined the group in the first place because participation was the only way she could keep her new baby; her other five children were in foster care. She came to all the meetings and dutifully planned the way she would raise this child—without the mistakes she had made in the past. Because she was such a willing pupil, Kathy and Tina gave her unusually explicit advice, including instructions about how to behave while pregnant and what to do when the baby was born. Only at the shower did I see Sandy exercise her recalcitrance and hold back from Tina and Kathy. And she was not alone in her "guerrilla" tactics.[30]

A number of us went to the beach early in the morning to set things up for the party. The shower was going to be a surprise and another member of the group, Shirley, would trick Sandy into coming. No sooner did we arrive than I saw signs of a form of behavior that would subsequently dominate the party. Two young, blond American soldiers sauntered by and the women instantly began making loud, sexually explicit remarks. The soldiers acted indifferent, and I was called upon: "go get them, they're your type, those *haole* boys." The women did not mind when I did nothing, and continued to hurl teasing insults at the young soldiers, who staunchly ignored the calls and stares. Already a tone of unrestrained sexuality framed the shower that was celebrating Sandy's new motherhood.

Eventually Sandy and Shirley drove up, and Sandy expressed her complete astonishment at the gathering. We spent a good deal of time opening the gifts people had brought, some practical—diapers and baby clothes—and some less so—perfumes and powders for Sandy. There was much discussion of babies, children, and families. After the gifts were opened and we finished eating, Kathy and Tina suggested a game of charades.

During the game, I had a sudden vision of the strategies Sandy and the other women used to resist conversion. The game was entirely sexualized; whatever the secret subject, the clues were graphically sexual. The women were totally unrestrained in their gestures and could well have been modern versions of the "loose and lax" women over whom 19th century mission wives blushed and despaired. Unlike the mission wives, however, Kathy and Tina constituted (with me) an appreciative audience, though they may have wondered about the impact of the weeks of purposeful consciousness-raising.

In fact, the open sexual expressiveness did not prompt Kathy and Tina into concern about a failure of the group to achieve its goals. What did prompt concern was another "rebellious" activity which occurred during the charades. Shirley had marijuana in her car and one by one women went off to smoke with her. When Sandy also left, Kathy and Tina grew serious and they reprimanded her as soon as she came back. Sandy only chuckled, knowing, she said, that the baby would be healthy and that a little *pakalolo* never hurt anyone. These "trivial" gestures, I began to conclude, constituted an alternative ideology and a sharp challenge to the model of womanhood Tina and Kathy offered the group. The significance of this form of resistance was brought home to me when I reviewed other incidents in which I had participated.

One afternoon, for instance, I hung around with Julie and Harmony. Julie had been a faithful member of the women's group and Harmony a somewhat cynical occasional participant. Both started off mentioning the "important things" that went on in the group. Julie said she wished there had been more "serious stuff" and less "gossip." She was working to put her life together, starting by leaving a husband who abused her. As the afternoon wore on and we became relaxed, Julie and Harmony moved on to reminisce about Harmony's affair with Julie's father. Together they conveyed the thick passion of this affair, as Harmony's detailed narrative bounced off Julie's appreciative chorus. Then talk turned to Julie's husband, an African-American. Making fun of her family for asking about the size of his penis, Julie proceeded to compare his penis with that of other men she had known. Both women insisted, too, on the woman's responsibility in sex: "you have to learn how to move your muscles down there." "I practice all the time," Julie claimed, and would not tell Harmony exactly how. And so the afternoon went on, with an increasing crescendo of sexual anecdotes.

Shirley was one of the ringleaders in the sexualization of talk and of gesture on all occasions. One afternoon in mid-summer, she and Marilyn told me how they had celebrated their "graduation" from the women's group. They had, they said, spent the whole afternoon on Hotel Street, a street well known for its bars and for its prostitutes. It was clear they had spent a lot of time in the bars, but not as clear what their sexual activities had been. Shirley played a close line on this, sometimes claiming at meetings that she had to make "extra income" through prostitution and sometimes merely implying that any sex was well worthwhile.

Not so much what they did or did not do, however, as their luscious narrative indicated to me that the graduation ceremony, like Sandy's shower and Julie's and Harmony's talk-story afternoon, represented an assertion of themselves as good *wahine* against the "women" Tina and Kathy hoped they would become.

The last, and saddest, story is that of Li-ann, a woman who seemed most thoroughly to incorporate the model Tina and Kathy sketched for the group. Li-ann had enrolled in a community college, was intending to bring her children home from her mother's house, and then to find a good job. She also had to break her attachment to Tom, a man whose power over her she was the first to admit, with pleasure as well as with distress. She never, as far as I knew, stopped seeing or sleeping with Tom; this was not an aspect of her behavior she could banish—and in the end, after a bitter fight, she stabbed him in the chest. He did not die; nor had her crime of passion won her a reprieve when last I heard. The tension in Li-ann's acceptance of a model that did not fit her life erupted in this last act. Her rebellion was against the discordance between *haole* and Hawaiian womanhood; her outburst represented an act of resistance to a situation in which competing messages were apparently irreconcilable.

Julie, Harmony, Shirley, and Marilyn more self-consciously resisted the message Kathy and Tina brought, and as *haole* outsider I served as a lightning rod for this resistance. Kathy and Tina were not such easy targets, inasmuch as their local style made them less "foreign."[31] But they did represent a *haole* agency and a *haole* perspective on womanhood, and I could be the stand-in for that element of their interactions with the women. The sexual anecdotes I heard, like the sexy charades performed for me, Kathy, and Tina, established an alternative model whose boundaries and content were impenetrable by any transforming experience imposed by any mission venture.

One can read back and assume a like resistance on the part of 19th century Hawaiian women. Behaviors that Mercy Whitney and Lucia Smith defined as backsliding or hypocrisy are better seen as gestures of resistance against a too-thorough reconstruction of identity. There is self-protection in the expedient docility and apparent cooperativeness one man, the nephew of a missionary, reported. When his aunt walked through the village, he wrote, "Bible and hymn books [were] brought conspicuously forward and the young girls hastily donned their chastest dresses and looks" (quoted in Grimshaw 1989b:42). The implication, of course, is that the aunt out of sight, the girls equally hastily "undonned" their chaste clothes and dropped their Bibles.

This and similar bits of evidence support my claim that Hawaiian women then, as now, had a firm sense of how far conversion could go and took steps to mark its limits. That those steps should involve an assertion of sexuality is not surprising, given both the culture of Hawaii and the dichotomy *haoles* created between sex and "true womanhood." To regard an assertion of sexuality as a form of resistance may be startling, yet it suits the theory that resistance will occur at a point of *both* cultural identification *and* obscurity from the public marketplace of competing ideologies. When the missionaries and the social workers decided to transform women, expecting to "raise" the nation, they also picked an aspect of behavior—sexuality—that more than they acknowledged represented the "state" of Hawaiian culture (see Sahlins 1985). To the extent, too, that missionaries and *haole* (or *haole*-influenced) social workers marked "sex" as a special domain, whether by being appalled or appreciative, they gave Hawaiian women a perfect opportunity to turn that into an arena of rebellion.

Kathy and Tina did not object to the sexual teasing and joking in the women's group, yet the fact that sex became the point of resistance suggests Sandy and the others detected the shadow text in all presentations of good womanhood emanating from *haole* culture. And like the girls observed by the missionary nephew, they reacted to it: Sandy, Shirley, Marilyn, Julie, and Harmony donned their "unchaste" clothing at the first opportunity. Their actions highlight the terms of the interaction between *haole* and Hawaiian: no less than their mission sisters did 20th century social workers assume "sex" made Hawaiian women vulnerable, at risk if not of the purity of their souls, then of the safety of their bodies. Alike in the spirit of resistance, though subject to drastically different relations of power, Hawaiian *wahine* in the 19th and in the 20th century refused to relinquish this aspect of their identity to the "foreign" visitors. The resistance indicates that messages about self-esteem are as hegemonic as instructions about domestic duty; in each case, the goal is not simply a change of behavior but the "conversion" to a new state of being. Shirley recognized, and refused, this when she celebrated her graduation on Hotel Street.

## Conclusion

> Yet, while collective action of a 'political' nature is consistently thwarted, the attempt to reassert control, to return to the world some form of coherence and tractability, continues. The effort is pursued through accessible implements that remain at the command of the 'powerless' and that speak to the contradictory location of the person in the world—the physical body and the practices which establish viable selfhood and a sense of relationship with a meaningful context. (Comaroff 1985:260)

Thus Comaroff argues for the importance of counterhegemonic movements that locate themselves in red nail polish, bright costumes, and drum-beat dances. In the Hawaiian instance, the implements of resistance are sexual gestures and anecdotes. Through such mechanisms, Comaroff argues, a protest is mounted against the vast implications of a colonial system; no uprising of this sort, she adds, fails.

Hers is an important, if problematic, argument and for me pushes further an issue Davenport raised about the Hawaiian cultural revolution (1969). At the end of that article he brings to center stage the personages through whom the encounter between *haole* and Hawaiian took shape. His emphasis on individual agency anticipates a mode of analysis that is currently dominant in anthropology: the significance of "actors" in the events and structures of history. Comaroff extends this acknowledgment of the role of personages by considering not only public behaviors and documented performances, but also slight gestures and "private" physical motions. Her book also allows us to see the seeds of conscious rebellion in apparently (to the actors as well as the observers) unconscious and spontaneous impulses, like inserting sex into every scene of a charade.

Yet her book lacks the tone of humility Davenport showed in almost everything he wrote—a respect for the persistence of struggle as part of the human condition. Thus Comaroff does not explore, as Bill might have, the significance of movements that *do* fail. Whether the women's group on the Waianae Coast represents a resistance that will eventually alter the dominant political and social system or whether the meetings are largely a relief from the stringencies of an ongoing struggle, remains a question. Whatever the answer in this particular case, data from such micro-encounters and "mundane practices" must constitute our next foci of inquiry if we are to understand resistance more thoroughly—and less ethnocentrically.

It is possible that the interactions I observed on the Waianae Coast contain the seeds of a successful resistance. In a 1990s Hawaii, poised on the edge of demands for Hawaiian sovereignty, the activities of a women's group constitute potentially powerful weapons. Out of "ventures" like that of Tina and Kathy may come the implements that will restore independence to the Hawaiian people and save the nation—but not as the missionaries dreamed.

## Acknowledgments

Beyond thanking him implicitly throughout the paper, I would like to thank Bill Davenport explicitly for teaching me a good part of the anthropology I know and do. Kathy and Tina and the women in the women's group must be thanked as well, for they welcomed me into some of the most personal aspects of their lives, and accepted my *haole* stumblings with good cheer. I learned, too, from attending David's men's group and from the several other gatherings to which I refer in the paper. In all cases, facilitators and participants were remarkably generous about the stranger in their midst. Sally Merry has been a helpful colleague and reader, as have the editors of the volume. The interpretations are my own.

## Notes

1. Robert Lowie was an early, though not the first, Western observer to express amazement at the way children were casually passed from hand to hand in Polynesian groups. Other studies have followed Lowie (1933); see also, for example, Carroll 1970, Brady 1976, Levy 1973, Howard 1974.

2. The Hawaiian sovereignty movement refers to a set of demands, including recognition of Hawaiian cultural autonomy, the return of lands appropriated by the American Government, and, in some instances, independence from the United States. Involving different groups, the "movement" has neither a tightly constructed platform nor a clear agenda for self-governance.

3. In *Ain't No Big Thing*, Howard (1974) discusses the importance of the affective and affiliative domain for an assertion of Hawaiian cultural identity.

4. A 1990 State Act "Relating to Family Support Centers" notes that because so many women are at work, Hawaiian families "are at high risk of becoming fragmented and dysfunctional...." (State of Hawaii 1990c).

5. One afternoon, I was startled to hear a friend call my driving "*haole*-style"— "because you went right through a stop sign," she explained.

6. My emphasis on the actors reflects a point Davenport (1969) made when he re-examined the role of Hawaiian personages in the early 19th century event known as the "cultural revolution."

7. Patricia Grimshaw's book on the Sandwich Islands mission (1989a) makes an effort to compensate for lack of data on Hawaiian responses by extracting these from the numerous documents left by the missionary wives. Others who write about mission movements point to the general lack of data on native responses, for example, Flemming 1992.

8. Beidelman's (1982) *Colonial Evangelism* was an important early work in this genre, an attempt to bring the issue of missionaries fully into anthropology; he mentions his significant predecessors. Much of the first work on missionaries treated Africa and Asia; recently, attention is being paid to missionary movements in the Pacific (e.g., Boutilier, Hughes and Tiffany 1978; Jolly and Macintyre 1989).

9. In his book, *Errand to the World*, Hutchison extends the meaning of "mission" when he claims: "The quandaries were real enough, and indeed intrinsic not just to this enterprise but, it would seem, to any venture in which one culture attempts to apply its ideals and technologies to the supposed benefit of another" (1987:13).

10. Hawaiian Homelands refers to the land granted people of Hawaiian ancestry under a 1921 U.S. Congressional Land Act; see, for example, MacKenzie 1991.

11. Social work training tended to be based on conventional American policies and principles, and this somewhat eroded the cultural differences likely to be present in any Hawaiian institution. A majority of social workers were *haole* or Japanese.

12. The notion of "local" culture is important, and signifies a way of talking (pidgin) and acting (Hawaiian-style) that are recognizable and often the basis for a common discourse.

13. Participation in the men's group, unlike the women's, was not voluntary. The participants had been sent to the group by the court in lieu of a jail sentence for a recently committed act of violence; they were only by chance connected with the women in the women's groups.

14. In her book *Sacred Queens and Women of Consequence*, Linnekin talks about *malama* (1990:80), a concept of responsible care that resembles David's conceptualization.

15. Talk-story is a classic Hawaiian form of narrative, rambling and anecdotal; it is described in Boggs 1985 and in Ito 1985.

16. I have borrowed from the distinction Hutchison (1987:185) makes between "transplanting" ideologies and "planting" new ideas.

17. In the early years of the mission, these women were called "wives" and not missionaries; this changed by the end of the 19th century.

18. Grimshaw's book, *Paths of Duty* (1989b), discusses the implications of Hawaiian class structure for the success (and failure) of the Sandwich Islands mission in more detail than I can do here (see also Linnekin 1990). That Hawaii was a deeply hierarchical society is not crucial to my broad point about the encounter between *haole* and Hawaiian. Missionary wives intended to make "good women" out of all women, queens and commoners alike.

19. Grimshaw (1989a) also suggests that watching Hawaiian children run around freely might have been hard on missionary wives who were adding conscientious care of their own children to the numerous burdens they already bore.

20. My participation in this semi-flirtatious kissing probably took me some way to being accepted by the women in the group. Later my friend Pamela told me that at that moment I did not seem "so *haole*."

21. That it gave its community representatives as much scope as it did shows the agency's sensitivity to the cultural diversity among its clients.

22. Jolly and Macintyre point out another complication: "As these women of New England themselves had problems in attaining their ideals of true womanhood, it is hardly surprising that Hawaiian women had even greater difficulties with such early attempts to recreate them as Christian wives" (1989:8).

23. The distinction between evangelization and social reform appears in most writings on missionaries, often with the recognition that such a distinction may be more one of theory than of practice; see, for example, Hutchison 1987, Flemming 1992.

24. That American children would somehow "catch" Hawaiianness may also have prompted the mission wives to send their older children home to New England, a common pattern by mid-century.

25. In *Paths of Duty*, Grimshaw suggests that the mission lost most of its energy by the second half of the 19th century.

26. Time-Out was established in the late 1980s as part of a more general church-related effort to prevent child abuse by giving parents respite from their children.

27. Afterwards, the teachers expressed disappointment over how few par-

ents had come, saying that was not always the case. I did not know either of the parents well enough to chat with them later; both left quickly when the session was over.

28. CPS has an overwhelmingly severe burden to bear in contemporary Hawaii, responsible as it is for protecting children from harm and from the "imminent threat of harm." Frequently, the only safe choice was to remove the child from her household right away.

29. See Modell 1993, on treatment of abused and neglected children in Hawaii.

30. I borrow the word from the epigraph to Comaroff's 1985 *Body of Power, Spirit of Resistance*, a book that has influenced my interpretation in this section.

31. That they were perceived as local, not fully *haole*, came out when the agency replaced them with, Pamela told me, "a real *haole* lady—stiff and uptight, her nose always in the air."

## References Cited

Beidelman, Thomas. 1982. *Colonial Evangelism*. Bloomington: Indiana University Press.

Boggs, Stephen. 1985. *Speaking, Relating, and Learning*. Norwood, N.J.: Ablex Publishing.

Boutilier, James A., Daniel T. Hughes, and Sharon W. Tiffany. 1978. *Mission, Church, and Sect in Oceania*. Lanham, Md.: University Press of America.

Brady, Ivan, ed. 1976. *Transactions in Kinship*. Honolulu: University of Hawaii Press.

Carroll, Vern, ed. 1970. *Adoption in Oceania*. Honolulu: University of Hawaii Press.

Comaroff, Jean. 1985. *Body of Power, Spirit of Resistance*. Chicago: University of Chicago Press.

Davenport, W.H. 1969. "Some Political and Economic Considerations of the 'Hawaiian Cultural Revolution'." *American Anthropologist* 71:1–19.

Flemming, Leslie A. 1992. "American Missionaries' Ideals for Women in North India, 1870–1930." In *Western Women and Imperialism*, ed. N. Chaudhuri and M. Strobel, pp. 191–206. Bloomington: Indiana University Press.

Grimshaw, Patricia. 1989a. *Paths of Duty: American Missionary Wives in Nineteenth-Century Hawaii*. Honolulu: University of Hawaii Press.

———. 1989b. "New England Missionary Wives, Hawaiian Women and 'The Cult of True Womanhood'." In *Family and Gender in the Pacific*, ed. M. Jolly and M. Macintyre, pp. 19–44. New York: Cambridge University Press.

Hawaiian Mission Children's Society Library. Records of the Maternal Association, Sandwich Islands Mission.

Howard, Alan. 1974. *Ain't No Big Thing*. Honolulu: University of Hawaii Press.

Hutchison, William R. 1987. *Errand to the World: American Protestant Thought and Foreign Missions*. Chicago: University of Chicago Press.

Ito, Karen. 1985. "Affective Bonds: Hawaiian Interrelationship of Self." In *Person, Self, and Experience*, ed. G. White and J. Kirkpatrick, pp. 301–27. Berkeley: University of California Press.

Jolly, Margaret, and Martha Macintyre. 1989. "Introduction." In *Family and Gender in the Pacific*, ed. M. Jolly and M. Macintyre, pp. 1–18. New York: Cambridge University Press.

Levy, Robert. 1973. *Tahitians: Mind and Experience in the Society Islands*. Chicago: University of Chicago Press.

Linnekin, Jocelyn. 1990. *Sacred Queens and Women of Consequence*. Ann Arbor, MI: University of Michigan Press.

Lowie, Robert. 1933. "Adoption." In *Encyclopedia of the Social Sciences*, ed. E.A. Seligman and A. Johnson, pp. 459–60. New York: Macmillan.

Mackenzie, M.K., ed. 1991. *Native Hawaiian Rights Handbook*. Honolulu: Native Hawaiian Legal Corporation, Office of Hawaiian Affairs.

Modell, Judith. 1993. "Rights to the Children: Foster Care and Social Reproduction in Hawaii." Paper delivered at the 92nd Annual Meeting of the American Anthropological Association.

Sahlins, Marshall. 1985. *Islands of History*. Chicago University of Chicago Press.

Sahlins, M., and T. Kirch. 1992. *Anahulu: The Anthropology of History in the Kingdom of Hawaii*. 2 vols. Chicago: University of Chicago Press.

State of Hawaii. 1990a. *Ka Pono O Na Keiki (State of the Children)*. Office of Children and Youth. Honolulu.

———. 1990b. *State Census*. Honolulu.

———. 1990c. *Session Laws of Hawaii, 15th State Legislature*. Honolulu.

# Empowered Women

*Laura Zimmer-Tamakoshi*

**Introduction**

Back in 1975, in his undergraduate course on Social Organization and through his paper "Nonunilinear Descent and Descent Groups" (1959), Bill Davenport introduced me to the idea that social principles as seemingly rigid as kinship were in fact variable in their restrictiveness and were ultimately dependent upon the strivings and goal-oriented behavior of individuals acting within particular social, economic, political, historical and environmental contexts.

This perspective on the relationship between structure and individual actions was reinforced in graduate school. At Bryn Mawr College, I read the works of Fredrik Barth (1966, 1967) and others (Belshaw 1968; Kapferer 1976) interested in social exchange and the role of the individual as a dynamic force in socio-cultural change. Intending to work in Papua New Guinea, I read the literature on Melanesia and studied the relationship between Melanesian social systems, exchange, and powerful or instrumental male and female actors (Brown 1972; Epstein 1969; Malinowski 1922; Salisbury 1962; A. Strathern 1971; M. Strathern 1972; Uberoi 1962; Weiner 1976). And I planned and went on to carry out research in Papua New Guinea on the effects of underdevelopment, labor migration, and inequality on the exchange relations and lives of the Gende, a group of Papua New Guinea Highlanders.

As a member of my dissertation committee, Bill continued to play a role in my work and intellectual development. With the Gende, I had encountered a people who were living on the edge of development—desiring it greatly, yet convulsed by the effects of unequal access to cash, primarily in the form of urban remittances (Zimmer 1986b). Spurred by opportunities to acquire more status and influence, land rights, and brides, or stung by humiliation and failed expectations, the relatives of prosperous migrants along with less fortunate villagers were engaged in intensely competitive exchanges. Alongside the competition, however, the Gende had created another system of exchange involving gambling with cards to redistribute cash from wealthy to poor and to mute the negative social effects of gross economic inequality (Zimmer 1986a, 1987a). Davenport's use of game theory (1960) helped me to understand the Gende's dual system of exchange. By continuing to seek glory and to judge one another in terms of performance in the old exchange system, Gende men and women were engaged in a losing game—a game in which the elderly could no longer rely on their children to repay their debts (Zimmer 1987b) and the proportion of aging bachelors was increasing as Gende women married more prosperous non-Gende husbands (Zimmer-Tamakoshi 1993a). By coming together to play cards in a way in which poorer villagers had as much or more chance of winning as did wealthier villagers, the Gende were bringing their game back into a mode in which no one player could for long dominate other players.

It was no accident that I went to Bryn Mawr. It was Bill who directed me there because of my interest in New Guinea and my need to be a part of a chain of empowering women and men. By going to Bryn Mawr, I was exposed to the importance of gender in our lives and the lives of the peoples we study. I was taught by Jane Goodale—a major contributor to the anthropology of gender with her *Tiwi Wives* (1971) and Kaulong studies (1980). I read the works of Jane's former students and also major contributors, Annette Weiner (1976) and Carol MacCormack (1980). And I went to classes and participated in conferences with yet other students of Jane's who are also involved in research on gender and gender issues.

When I went back to Papua New Guinea in 1986 to teach at the University of Papua New Guinea and to continue my study of the Gende people, both Bill and Jane urged me to pay closer attention to what was happening with Gende women as they experienced social change. With ample opportunity to study not only Gende women but others as well, I have since written about Papua New Guinea women from a variety of perspectives: as young husband hunters (Zimmer-Tamakoshi 1993a), urban homemakers (Zimmer-Tamakoshi, In press), working wives and members of the educated elite (Rosi and Zimmer-Tamakoshi 1993), unequal partners in development (Zimmer-Tamakoshi n.d.), victims of domestic violence and rape (Zimmer 1990), and politicians and women's rights advocates (Zimmer-Tamakoshi 1993b). In most instances, the women were actively engaged in changing and improving the circumstances of their lives. Rarely did I observe women blindly following society's dictates.

## Women, Age, and Power

In the 1970s representations of women as powerful social actors acting on their own behalf began to replace earlier views of women as primarily the helpmates of men. In Goodale's *Tiwi Wives* (1971), the portrayal of young and old females as pawns in men's efforts to achieve power through marriage brokerage and controlling women's labor was modified by evidence that older women achieve considerable power and autonomy in Tiwi society in much the same way as men—through increasing knowledge, sophistication, and control over younger persons (daughters, younger co-wives, sons, and younger husbands).

Other works on women also support a varied picture of women's lives and the sources of power for women (MacCormack and Strathern 1980; Nash and Safa 1976; Ortner and Whitehead 1981; M. Strathern 1987). There is a large literature, for example, on female office holders and women's involvement in anticolonial protest movements in Africa and elsewhere (Etienne and Leacock 1980; Hafkin and Bay 1976; MacCormack 1980). Weiner's work on Trobriand exchange (1976) shows how Trobriand women use their production of banana leaf wealth to reclaim land rights compromised by men's exchange activities, in the process showing themselves to be women of value and influence. A collection of essays on widows in Africa shows that these women are not passive pawns in male transactions governing widow inheritance (Potash 1986). And Janet MacGaffey's work on women in Zaire shows how women migrants use a variety of survival strategies including trade and informal sector jobs to achieve a measure of independence from men (1988).

In a collection of articles focused on middle-aged women, Virginia Kerns and Judith Brown present convincing cross-cultural data on the widespread phenomenon of women acquiring greater status and freedom from former restrictions as they leave off childbearing and childcare responsibilities and reach middle age (1985). One aspect of the change in women's status is older women's greater geographic mobility as their sexuality becomes less dangerous or in need of protection (Brown and Kerns 1985:3). Older women acquire increased authority over younger individuals, including their children's spouses, and become eligible for special statuses and recognition beyond the household (Brown and Kerns 1985:4–5). In some societies, for example, older women—but not younger women—may become holy women, midwives, and curers.

Looking at age stratification more generally, Nancy Foner surveyed the literature on age inequalities based on an individual's location in a particular age group or life course category (1984). Like Kerns and Brown, Foner noted that unequal access to valued social roles and rewards increases for both men and women during or after middle age. In a paper based on her research in the Highlands of Papua New Guinea, Jeanette Dickerson-Putman (n.d.) explores the nature of the Bena Bena's age stratification system. She looks at how Bena Bena culture affords older women access to valued social roles and rewards and allows them to exert control over the lives and opportunities of younger women. Bena Bena women are considered social adults when they reach menopause and when they have demonstrated productivity and commitment in culturally approved roles. Aging and social adulthood give women greater authority within their own households. They can control the labor of younger women, and they are consulted in marriage arrangements and in the distribution of resources. Social adulthood also allows women to participate in a wider range of extra-domestic activities. As curers and midwives older women are paid for their knowledge about birth, contraception, and abortion. They also play an important role in male initiation. The most important role that an older woman plays, however, is that of women's representative in community affairs.

The distinction between a woman's physical age and her productivity and commitment to culturally appropriate roles is an important one in Melanesia. In a paper in the Brown and Kerns volume (1985), Dorothy Counts argues that attention should focus on a component that is implicit in many explanations of women's greater domestic, political, and economic authority in their middle and later years: namely, the notion of responsibility. In her study of Lusi women in West New Britain, Papua New Guinea, Counts found that the increased prestige, authority, and autonomy of older Lusi women "does not represent a radical departure from her way of life as a younger woman. Neither can it be explained as being a result of biological or social changes associated with menopause..." (1985:50). Rather, with the maturity of her children and the decline of her parents, a women becomes responsible for herself, her younger kin and affines, her dependent parents, and the maintenance of society (1985:50). Lusi women are judged by the contributions they make to themselves and others, not by age per se. A Lusi woman who is lazy in fulfilling her responsibilities or married to an unimportant husband is as unlikely to command others' respect as a new bride.

## Women, Age, and Power Among the Gende of Papua New Guinea

Like other New Guinea Highlanders, the Gende people living in the mountains in southern Madang Province practice patrilineal descent, reside partrilocally as a rule, and obtain brides by giving brideprice to the women's families. In the villages, the division of labor is much the same as it was in the past with, for example, men clearing the bush and forests for their wives to plant large sweet potato gardens and raise pigs—the most valued exchange item in the Highlands. Also in keeping with other Highland societies, the Gende's gender ideology—from a Gende male's perspective—is such that men are considered superior to women in intelligence, strength, trustworthiness, and political ability. Even so, and even though some Gende women also subscribe to these beliefs, Gende women may achieve great influence and respect through their participation in the Gende exchange system.

Like the Lusi and Bena Bena, the Gende base their age stratification system more on achievement than age. Thus, as persons age they are expected to take on more responsibility in the affairs of both younger and elderly persons. Later, as they approach middle age, their contributions to group affairs are measured in the number of brideprices they have contributed to, in their exchange performances at competitive pig feasts, and in funerary exchanges on behalf of deceased kin. Persons who excel in exchange are recognized as Big Men and Good Women and are the center of activities in both village and town. Persons who fail to make much of a contribution are judged to be rubbish persons or like children relying on others to help them. Past middle age, men and women are concerned to help others so that someone will mourn their deaths and see that they are given proper burials and appropriate post-funeral rituals and sacrifices (Zimmer 1987b). Responsible generosity, then, helps build and maintain a base of power and influence for individuals as they progress through the life-cycle.

## The Gende Exchange System and Life Cycle

What structure there is to Gende society is the result of an elaborate system of exchange. At its core are all those exchanges pertinent to successive stages in the life cycle and social development of the individual. Each stage is marked by the exchange of pigs and other material goods or services. As conceived by the Gende, this process of exchange carries the individual from a state of potential being through states of becoming human (*wana tizhi*), being human (*wana minanua*), becoming an ancestor (*poroi tizhi*), and being an ancestral spirit (*poroi minanua*).

Through life, but particularly in the becoming human and becoming an ancestor stages, an individual needs others to invest wealth in him or her. Thus, when an individual reaches physical maturity, he or she is expected to begin reciprocating the assistance of parents and others who have helped him or her through the earlier stages of childhood and marriage, by in turn *being human* and helping them make the transition from living persons to benevolent ancestors. They are also expected to invest wealth in their own and others' children's development.

## Becoming Human

When a baby first responds to those around it, it is said that he or she is "becoming human." Long before the child was conceived, however, its grandparents and others prepared the way for it to be born and to prosper. Its mother's relatives, for example, had looked after the mother throughout her childhood, made sure that her puberty rites were carried out in a way that she would become a healthy and fertile adult, and instructed her in the duties and restrictions of a proper wife and mother. On the father's side, it is expected that his relatives would have given an appropriately large brideprice to the mother's relatives in recognition of the care they had given to her and to ensure that the mother's relatives and clan ancestors do not bring harm to the baby and any other children born of the union.

Soon after a baby is born, its parents give a small feast to celebrate the child's safe delivery and to show appreciation for the birth attendants and those men and women who paid the mother's brideprice and thereby helped to bring this event to pass. A year or two later a much bigger feast is arranged in further recognition of the mother's kin's contribution to the birth. Just as failure to pay a woman's full brideprice may bring into question the clan affiliation of any children she bears her husband, so too does the failure to pay childwealth—at least with the first child—raise doubts about a clan's rights over a child.

As soon as they are weaned, boys and girls begin to learn the tasks and behaviors appropriate to their sex. While gangs of little boys roam the village, playing games of war or marbles, swimming in the river, or hunting in the surrounding bush, girls help their mothers by tending younger siblings while their mothers go off to work in the gardens. When they are older, girls help their mothers in their gardens and, in some cases, look after gardens their fathers or brothers have prepared especially for them, raising pigs for their brothers' future brideprices or their own dowry.

While boys go through a lengthy male initiation into their fathers' clans, Gende girls participate in shorter but equally important rituals beginning with the onset of menstruation. Puberty rituals include seclusion, food taboos, injunctions such as sleeping with their legs tied together with ropes so they will not roam in the night, and much lecturing on love magic and the appropriate behavior for married women. Women say that puberty rituals are comparable to male initiation. For just as boys are shown the secret flutes of their clan and learn of the flutes' power, so too are girls taught about their own special powers, powers they must learn to control for socially approved ends. Some of these powers include women's ability to give birth to children (or not to give birth), women's powers of seduction, and women's magic and sorcery. Women's sorcery, acquired individually or by inheritance from an older woman, is especially feared by Gende men as potentially more powerful than their own.

The culminating event of a puberty ceremony is the killing of pigs. The same people mobilized for her brother's initiation also participate in the feast held at the end of a girl's seclusion in the menstrual hut. These people will include her parents, her father's brothers and their wives, and usually close kin in her mother's clan and her father's sisters' husbands' clans as well. Furthermore, just as a young man's future brideprice-contributors pay close attention to his potential for being a strong and generous man, so too will the number of participants at a girl's puberty ceremony depend upon her performance in working in the gardens, helping her mother and other women in their gardens, and developing the skills necessary to be a mature woman. The number of pigs that participants sacrifice at the end of her puberty ceremony are a mark of their estimation of her value and will help her attract a good husband.

## Being Human and Becoming an Ancestor

With marriage there is a shift in an individual's life from being a recipient to becoming a donor. When men and women enter their productive and reproductive years—i.e., are showing themselves to have become true human beings—investment in them lessens and becomes a matter of lending support when needed or investing in an especially promising political future of some young man or woman.

In the early years of their marriage, a husband's and wife's primary obligation to one another is to work together to raise pigs to repay the investments other persons have made in them. This obligation falls most heavily on the woman, who is from another group and has been paid for with many pigs and other forms of wealth. To help her get started, a young woman's mother and mother's sisters give her a small herd of pigs as a kind of dowry on the day she leaves home to move to her husband's place. Added to these pigs may be others the young wife has raised on her own behalf.

The most important repayment goes to the young wife's in-laws for their contributions to her brideprice. Among the Gende, this repayment is a formal part of the Gende exchange system and is called *tupoi*, literally to give back the pigs. Fulfilling the *tupoi* obligation, a woman redeems herself from indebtedness to others and becomes a more independent actor in Gende affairs. Evidence for this independence is found in the Gende divorce laws whereby a woman who has repaid her brideprice and any other lesser debts to her husband's people may take all of her pigs with her when she leaves her husband. More importantly, a woman's in-laws treat her with greater respect once she has done *tupoi*, and both she and her husband are sought out for their opinions on matters concerning the husband's group.

Far from being a time to rest on their laurels, after *tupoi* is made a couple are expected to take on the responsibilities of mature adults and to sponsor exchanges which will advance the group's interests. One of the most important interests of the group is the birth of children and their affiliation with the husband's clan. In order to maintain a balance between themselves and others, a clan needs to maintain its numbers, to have fully committed members who will participate in inter-clan pig competitions and, in the past, warfare and the defense of clan territory and other clan rights.

A child's clan affiliation is made more certain by the giving of childwealth to the mother's people. In the past it was expected that a child's parents would pay all or most of the childwealth payment. Today, however, many couples have children before they have made *tupoi*, a fact associated with larger (and therefore harder to repay) brideprices and the unwillingness of many couples to wait to begin sexual relations until after they have made *tupoi*. Often, other clan members must step in and pay the childwealth debt for a young couple.

For men and women who are ambitious, paying the debts of other couples is an investment opportunity. Placing children (their own and others') in their debt by investing pigs in their various rites of passage—birth, puberty, and marriage—men and women may accumulate a large fund of stored wealth which the children will be obligated to repay when they are grown. Among the Gende, the highest acclaim attaches to those individuals who are able—through years of hard work and careful investment—to contribute the most pigs to group-sponsored pig feasts and other ceremonial events. Most often this is accomplished by becoming the 'mother' or 'father' of many individuals, who reciprocate past investments when the donors are ready to sponsor large feasts. When Big Men and Good Women are praised for their contributions to group affairs, most often they are praised as "our mother," "our father."

In addition to clan prestige and strength, a compelling reason for investing in children is so that one will be taken care of in old age and mourned in death. When persons are nearing death or have already died, it is also expected that any residual debts associated with their past exchange activities will be honored, by themselves, by persons who are indebted to them, and/or by persons who wish to invest in their 'ancestors.' By investing wealth in persons who are soon to be or are already dead, individuals secure the good will of ancestral parents. They may also lay claims on lands the deceased had rights over during their lifetime. This is so whether or not the individual is male or female, since among the Gende both men and women have potential rights in their parents' lands, rights which must, however, be paid for. When a man dies, for example, his children must pay off any lingering debts he may have to his mother's, wife's, or sister's husband's clan(s) in order to have clear access to any lands he used. Usually it is the man's sons and daughters-in-law who host the death payment feast, but if they are too poor to do so, his brothers or brother's sons or even his sisters may do so. Likewise, when a woman dies, it is normally her sons and her son's wives who give the bulk of the death payments to her brothers. This is so that any rights to her husband's land the woman may have earned through her hard work and the investments of her clan in her exchange activities will pass to her sons and not accrue to her brothers' sons. It is interesting to note, of course, this limiting aspect of patrilineality: that in helping her husband to secure his clan lands by paying off his parents' debts (and thereby building a base of power for herself in her husband's group), a woman undercuts claims her brothers and their wives (who are very probably her husband's sisters) may have in the same land. By pitting women against their sisters-in-law in this way, Gende society (perhaps other patrilineal societies as well) put an extra burden on women and their efforts to achieve security and full autonomy. To have it both ways, a woman must work very hard and give large death payments at the deaths of both her husband's and her own parents.

## Empowered and Empowering Women

It was obvious from the start of my fieldwork that Gende women were neither pawns in men's power games nor necessarily the beaten-down and oppressed victims of male chauvinism. Of all the Gende I met, teenage girls were the cockiest, particularly girls who had been through their puberty ceremonies and were being sought after by admirers. Undoubtedly today's higher brideprices add to young women's sense of self-importance. But, even young men whose families can afford to pay large brideprices were rattled by the prospects of securing the interest and hand of the girl of their choice and of settling down to work with that woman to fulfill the debts of childhood and to build reputations as responsible and generous persons. Older women were outspoken and often disgruntled about how hard they worked to help their husbands make names for themselves. They were also the most aggressive and vocal, however, in spurring their husbands on to greater effort in all kinds of exchange activities by reminding them of the perils of old age and death without others to help take care of them or to mourn their deaths. And significantly, few men were foolish enough to openly disparage their wives' contributions; even Big Men publicly acknowledged their wives' efforts and conferred with them on the best strategies in distributing pork or giving away money to exchange partners.

The structure of Gende society affords women opportunities to empower both themselves and others. Some women make more of these opportunities than do others, and successful women are women who cooperate with both men *and* women to empower themselves, their daughters, or other family members. At a girl's puberty ceremony, older women are in the forefront in judging a girl's capabilities and deciding on the number of pigs that will be sacrificed for her. They also invest quite a bit of time and energy into educating the girl on being a successful wife, daughter-in-law, and mother, and—if she is deemed worthy—a powerful sorceress. Older men are also present in the proceedings, and their male viewpoints are sought out to advise the girl about how to keep young husbands attentive and hard-working. For their part, young women must earn the respect of older women as well as impress older men that they are capable of much hard work and generosity in addition to keeping their husbands from straying.

Similarly, in redeeming her brideprice in *tupoi* payments, a woman earns the right to control her own production and how it is used. She also, however, has more than herself to thank, beginning with those women who started her off in married life with a dowry herd, and her husband and any others who helped clear gardens for her to plant sweet potatoes to feed her pigs and family.

How hard a woman chooses to work and for whom is crucial to both men's and women's interests. Thus, not only will her husband clear gardens for her, but others will also help her: unmarried youths by clearing additional gardens in return for future brideprice pigs; young women by sharing in the planting of these gardens in return for various kinds of support; and older men and women by looking after some of the woman's pigs in their own small gardens in return for future care and funerary payments.

Investing her pigs and labor in getting others through the various stages and challenges of life, a woman accrues prestige and influence. As the center of a network of helping hands—the unmarried youths, young women, older persons and others—she may even accumulate enough indebtedness to her to become a major player in a large pig feast. On the occasion of the first pig feast I witnessed in Yandera village, for example, women shared the stage with men, directing the feeding and housing of numerous guests and exchange partners; dressing in their best feathers and traditional clothing to lead their pig herds to the slaughter; and critically observing and commenting on their husbands' distribution of the cooked pork. My very favorite memory of that time—captured in a slide—is one in which the biggest Big Man in Yandera village is orating in front of a huge pile of cooked pork alongside of which are squatting or standing his three wives, his widowed mother, and several of his brothers' wives—all of whom are singularly unimpressed with his speech and more interested to see that he distributes the pork as they see fit.

Finally, if a woman has been active throughout her middle and later years, she will be attended to and revered in old age and death. Even daughters-in-law who may not feel kindly disposed towards their mother-in-law in view of their sometimes competing interests will respect her as a "mother" or "ancestor" of their children's and husbands' group. And although it is common for older women to spend considerable time visiting their brothers—sometimes for weeks or months—their sons and grandchildren are usually anxious for them to return home where they can look after them properly and avoid a situation in which their mother or grandmother dies while she is away and feels resentment towards them after death. But unless an older woman has exhibited powerful behavior through years of hard work and sacrifice, such threats would be powerless.

## Conclusion

With the exception of Elizabeth Faithorn's view on female life and male-female relations among the Kafe (1976), earlier perspectives on Papua New Guinea Highlands women viewed them as segregated from and subservient to males, and portrayed male-female relations as tense and antagonistic (cf. Brown 1972; Glasse and Meggitt 1969; Langness 1967; Meggitt 1964; Salisbury 1962; M. Strathern 1972, among others). By contrast, my portrayal shows women actively engaged in exchange activities and working with other women and men to achieve their own and mutual ends.

Such a view is necessary if we are to make sense of women's situations and actions in today's changing world. Young Gende women, for example, are often willing to leave their villages to live in town where they take their chances marrying more prosperous but foreign husbands in order to get the higher brideprices their families expect for them (Zimmer-Tamakoshi 1993a). And older women, although they will often work very hard to raise brideprice pigs for their sons if they think there is a possibility they will attract a suitable wife, are today more likely to help young men who are educated and/or have landed lucrative jobs in town, even if it means setting aside the interests of their own sons, since it is necessary to invest in young men who will someday be able to reciprocate that help (Zimmer 1987b).

It is also significant that in the literature there is little understanding of the full measure of what brideprice and its repayment means to women. For Gende women, having a large brideprice means having a big network of supporters—women and men who have already invested in her puberty rites, are repaid by her brideprice, and will undoubtedly be willing to invest in her in the future. It also means having a large *tupoi* obligation to fulfill. But more importantly, it is the means by which a woman enters into the politics and social life of the larger Gende community. By working her way through the system she can amass considerable influence and glory. It is the same for men. They are indebted to their supporters for their male initiation ceremonies and brideprice contributions. And like women, they can work their way through these debts and come out on top after years of hard work and cooperation with spouses, parents, in-laws, children, and others of both sexes.

## References Cited

Barth, Fredrik. 1966. *Models of Social Organization*. Royal Anthropological Institute of Great Britain and Ireland Occasional Paper, No. 23. London.

———. 1967. "On the Study of Social Change." *American Anthropologist* 69:661–69.

Belshaw, Cyril. 1968. "Theoretical Problems in Economic Anthropology." In *Social Organization: Essays Presented to Raymond Firth*, ed. Maurice Freedman, pp. 25–42. Chicago: Aldine Atherton.

Brown, Judith K., and Virginia Kern, eds. 1985. *In Her Prime: A New View of Middle-Aged Women*. South Hadley, Mass.: Bergin and Garvey.

Brown, Paula. 1972. *The Chimbu: A Study of Change in the New Guinea Highlands*. Cambridge: Schenkman.

Counts, Dorothy Ayers. 1985. "Tamparonga: 'The Big Women' of Kaliai (Papua New Guinea)." In *In Her Prime*, ed. Judith K. Brown and Virginia Kerns, pp. 49–64. South Hadley, Mass.: Bergin and Garvey.

Davenport, William H. 1959. "Nonunilinear Descent and Descent Groups." *American Anthropologist* 61:557–72.

———. 1960. *Jamaican Fishing: A Game Theory Analysis*. Yale University Publications in Anthropology, No. 59. New Haven.

Dickerson-Putman, Jeanette. n.d. "Old Women at the Top: An Exploration of Age Stratification Among Bena Bena Women." Paper presented at the ASAO session on Women, Age and Influence in Oceania, New Orleans, February 1992.

Epstein, A.L. 1969. *Matupit: Land, Politics and Change Among the Tolai of New Britain*. Canberra: Australian National University Press.

Etienne, Mona, and Eleanor Leacock, eds. 1980. *Women and Colonization*. New York: J.F. Bergin.

Faithorn, Elizabeth. 1976. "Women as Persons: Aspects of Female Life and Male-Female Relations Among the Kafe." In *Man and Woman in the New Guinea Highlands*, ed. P. Brown and G. Buchbinder, pp. 86–95. Washington, D.C.: American Anthropological Association (Special Publication Number 8).

Foner, Nancy. 1984. *Ages in Conflict: A Cross-Cultural Perspective on Inequality Between Old and Young*. New York: Columbia University Press.

Glasse, R.M., and M.J. Meggitt. 1969. *Pigs, Pearlshells and Women*. Englewood Cliffs, N.J.: Prentice-Hall.

Goodale, Jane. 1971. *Tiwi Wives*. Seattle: University of Washington Press.

———. 1980. "Gender, Sexuality and Marriage: A Kaulong Model of Nature and Culture." In *Nature, Culture and Gender*, ed. C. MacCormack and M. Strathern, pp. 119–42. Cambridge: Cambridge University Press.

Hafkin, Nancy J., and Edna G. Bay. 1976. *Women in Africa*. Stanford: Stanford University Press.

Hart, C.W.M., and Arnold R. Pilling. 1960. *The Tiwi of North*

*Australia*. New York: Holt, Rinehart and Winston.

Kapferer, Bruce, ed. 1976. *Transaction and Meaning: Directions in the Anthropology of Exchange and Symbolic Behavior*. Philadelphia: ISHI.

Langness, L.L. 1967. "Sexual Antagonism in the New Guinea Highlands: A Bena Bena Example." *Oceania* 37:161–77.

MacCormack, Carol. 1980. "From Proto-Social to Adult: A Sherbro Transformation." In *Nature, Culture and Gender*, ed. C. MacCormack and M. Strathern, pp. 95–119. Cambridge: Cambridge University Press.

MacCormack, Carol, and Marilyn Strathern. 1980. *Nature, Culture and Gender*. Cambridge: Cambridge University Press.

MacGaffey, Janet. 1988. "Evading Male Control: Women in the Second Economy in Zaire." In *Patriarchy and Class: African Women in the Home and the Workforce*, ed. Sharon B. Stichter and Jane L. Parpart, pp. 161–77. Boulder, Colo.: Westview Press.

Malinowski, Bronislaw. 1922. *Argonauts of the Western Pacific*. New York: E.P. Dutton.

Meggitt, M.J. 1964. "Male-Female Relationships in the Highlands of Australian New Guinea." In *New Guinea: The Central Highlands*, ed. J. B. Watson, pp. 204–24. Special publication of *American Anthropologist* 66(4), Part 2. Menasha, Wis.: American Anthropological Association.

Nash, June, and Helen Safa. 1976. *Sex and Class in Latin America*. New York: Praeger.

Ortner, Sherry B., and Harriet Whitehead. 1981. *Sexual Meanings*. New York: Cambridge University Press.

Potash, Betty. 1986. *Widows in African Societies: Choices and Constraints*. Stanford: Stanford University Press.

Rosi, Pamela, and Laura Zimmer-Tamakoshi. 1993. "Love and Marriage Among the Educated Elite in Port Moresby." In *The Business of Marriage: Transformations in Oceanic Matrimony*, ed. Rick Marksbury, pp. 175–204. Pittsburgh: University of Pittsburgh Press.

Salisbury, Richard F. 1962. *From Stone to Steel*. Melbourne: Melbourne University Press.

Strathern, Andrew. 1971. *The Rope of Moka: Big Men and Ceremonial Exchange in Mount Hagen, New Guinea*. Cambridge: Cambridge University Press.

Strathern, Marilyn. 1972. *Women In Between; Female Roles in a Male World: Mount Hagen, New Guinea*. New York: Seminar Press.

Strathern, Marilyn, ed. 1987. *Dealing with Inequality: Analysing Gender Relations in Melanesia and Beyond.* Cambridge: Cambridge University Press.

Uberoi, J.P. Singh. 1962. *Politics of the Kula Ring: An Analysis of the Findings of Bronislaw Malinowski.* Manchester: Manchester University Press.

Weiner, Annette B. 1976. *Women of Value, Men of Renown: New Perspectives in Trobriand Exchange.* Austin: University of Texas Press.

Zimmer, Laura J. 1986a. "Card Playing Amongst the Gende: A System for Keeping Money and Social Relationships Alive." *Oceania* 56:245–63.

———. 1986b. *The Losing Game—Exchange, Migration and Inequality Among the Gende People of Papua New Guinea.* Ann Arbor, Michigan: University Microfilms International.

———. 1987a. "Playing at Being Men." *Oceania* (Special Issue: Gambling With Cards in Melanesia and Australia) 58:22–37.

———. 1987b. " 'Who Will Bury Me?' The Plight of Childless Elderly Among the Gende." *Journal of Cross-Cultural Gerontology* 2:61–77.

———. 1990. "Sexual Exploitation and Male Dominance in Papua New Guinea." In *Human Sexuality in Melanesian Cultures*, ed. Joel Ingebrittson, pp. 250–67. *Point*, Series No. 14. Papua New Guinea: Melanesian Institute.

Zimmer-Tamakoshi, Laura J. 1993a. "Bachelors, Spinsters and 'Pamuk Meris'." In *The Business of Marriage: Transformations in Oceanic Matrimony*, ed. Rick Marksbury, pp. 83–104. Pittsburgh: University of Pittsburgh Press.

———. 1993b. "Nationalism and Sexuality in Papua New Guinea." *Pacific Studies* 16 (December): 61–97.

———. In press. "Papua New Guinea Women in Town: Housewives, Homemakers, and Household Managers." In *Modern PNG Society*, ed. Laura Zimmer-Tamakoshi. Bathurst, Australia: Crawford House Press.

———. n.d. "Constraints on Women and Development in Papua New Guinea." Paper presented at the SFAA and ASAO Sessions on Women and Development in Oceania, Memphis and New Orleans, 1992.

# Exchanging Sisters Is Not a Game

*James G. Flanagan*

My title is a play on Davenport's seminal *Jamaican Fishing* paper (1960) and is in no way intended to suggest either that I will apply game theory models to the analysis of sister-exchange or that I reject the possibility of such application. It is intended to convey a general feeling of intellectual indebtedness that one always feels towards scholars whose innovation and insight have helped shape the current state of the discipline.

My use of the term "game" here is perhaps closer to that in Daniel Bradburd's 1984 article where, with reference to the Komachi nomads of southern Iran, he employs the term "game" to denote, essentially, a field of play or a locus of action. Following Bourdieu (1977), Bradburd discusses the two types of rules that impinge on Komachi marriage practice: "those about who may play the game—proscriptions and preferences; and those about how to play the game—the accepted practice of courtship" (1984:740).

Nor, indeed, can I undertake a direct comparison of ethnographic situations. Davenport's significant corpus on Santa Cruz concerns a series of societies whose subsistence is sea-based, who are involved in strictly and hierarchically defined inter-societal relations, including the exchange of women, and whose internal political relations are far more "complex" than those I encountered on the northern fringe of the New

Guinea Highlands. My own experience with the Wovan involves a society that is small-scale, of low population density, whose subsistence is based on pig herding and swiddening, and whose stated rules of sister exchange and parallel-cousin marriage, while subverted on a regular basis by the unruliness of women, requires that they conform to most classical anthropological definitions of an 'egalitarian' society. My comparison, ultimately then, is intended to emulate Davenport's rigor and clarity (a task at which I will undoubtedly fail) while drawing what lessons I can from contrastive ethnographic circumstances.

## The Highlands' Fringe

"Meri, em i samting bilong bisnis, olsem kakaruk." Thus spoke Bagami, one of the younger men, in pidgin, one night in the heat of a series of complaints about young Wovan women. These complaints centered particularly on the women's desire for more sophisticated Kopon and Kalam husbands, and their often derisive rejections of young Wovan men's advances that frequently implied, or were taken to imply, biological inadequacy. We lack here the poetics of Butaritari as presented by Lambert (1983:180–81), where daughters are likened to "cultivated taro" which requires careful attention but will be consumed by someone else, and sons to "uncultivated taro" which requires minimal attention and will be retained for family consumption. "We marry our sisters" after all is a standard Wovan description of marriage patterns. There is no outside consumer. There is, instead, the disruption caused by endogamous marriage or rather the transacting of endogamous marriages and the constant battle to keep everything equal, at least between men (Flanagan 1988a).

"Marriage," as Mahir Saul suggests with regard to the Bobo of West Africa, is "a social field in which authority is played out, divergent perspectives maintained and actions contested" (1989:57). While the institutional context within which the Bobo transact marriages is very different from that of the Wovan on the Highlands' fringe (I persevere in my usage despite alternative putative 'ethnonyms' [see Comrie 1987]), the behavioral possibilities are very similar.

The Wovan are a small-scale society practicing sister exchange. Community endogamy provides an alternative to establishing lasting alliance relationships. The Wovan, indeed, continue to convert affinity into consanguinity by confining the circle of recognized affines to the immediate kin of the spouse. By strategies of genealogical manipulation, the Wovan maintain a system that, at least normatively, conforms to one of "straight sister exchange" (Meller 1980), although this system is continually subverted by the actions of unruly women (Flanagan 1988b; see also McDowell 1990, and below, for similar situations in Bun).

"The logic of direct-exchange is that only a woman can be exchanged for a woman," as Marilyn Strathern has noted (Strathern 1985:197). Such systems are, necessarily, underpinned by an ideology of egalitarianism. In Wovan whether we are dealing with the exchange of pork, shells, or persons, the underlying desire is for reciprocity of like for like, immediate or delayed. However, unlike shell exchanges, where one must be constantly aware of the possibility of being unable to procure a "like shell," persons can always be found to fulfill appropriate categorical positions and, thus, continue exchange processes. But specific persons may themselves compete to affect their categorical label.

A discussion of brother/sister exchange in Wovan is, necessarily, a discussion of the position of women in Wovan society, particularly the position of younger—that is, marriageable—women. Young women in Wovan enjoy considerable freedom of movement. They are largely freed from domestic chores and, in groups, spend considerable amounts of time away from their natal homesteads. They are spoken of by their male counterparts, and indeed present themselves, as sexually aggressive.

Indeed, discussions with young (marriageable) men almost inevitably turn to the derogation of female sexuality and the fear of women (both spiritually, in terms of pollution, and secularly, in terms of seduction) (Flanagan 1988b). In their characterization of what they termed "brideservice societies," Collier and Rosaldo see them as societies where "individuals are autonomous, adults being in no position to command others, to a large extent controlling the foodstuffs they acquire and experiencing considerable freedom to withdraw from undesirable interactions" (Collier and Rosaldo 1981:279, 289; Strathern 1985:196). The Wovan conform in most respects, with the significant exception of performing brideservice, to Collier and Rosaldo's model. But, of course, that exception is of major import.

Young women have significant control over their own marital careers and they exercise this control regularly. Wovan women marry later than their neighbors. Fathers and brothers may attempt to arrange marriages, but a woman has ultimate control over whom she *will* marry. This autonomy is a woman's major weapon in interpersonal politics, and while each man wants to arrange his "sister's" marriage and, thereby, ensure his own marital career, each also wants to be the object of someone else's sister's desire. "Adolescence," for a Wovan woman, as I've said elsewhere (1988b:14), "is not some limbo between childhood boredom and marital drudgery. It is, rather, the staging ground for an entire career during which she establishes her reputation and asserts her identity."

Cases similar to Wovan are easily found in the New Guinea literature. The Ilahita Arapesh manipulate genealogies to provide fictive sisters for those men who are without women in the appropriate genealogical category (Tuzin 1976:131). Confronting a similar situation in Bun, Nancy McDowell (1990) re-imports Sahlins's New Guinea-derived Hawaiian model (1986) to traverse again ground originally explored by Chowning and Goodenough (1971) and Watson (1970), among others. This is not to suggest that her approach is any less productive for all that. Indeed by focusing on "performative structures" in contrast to "prescriptive structures," McDowell elucidates significant elements of the conversion of kin into appropriate units of exchange or marriage partners, aligning her analysis more closely with "native perceptions" of "native practice" than prescriptive approaches, which see only the discordance between externally conceptualized *structure* and externally perceived *event*, would allow. In doing so, McDowell's analysis goes some way toward meeting Schneider's demand that we differentiate between "functionally significant" and "culturally significant" units of analysis (1992: 630) and returns our focus to the emergent nature of social relations (as Wagner has done for communities in Daribi [1988:59], and indeed as G.H. Mead [1934] called for in the 1920s).

On the other side of the Central Highlands, Bruce Knauft has described a situation among the Gebusi very similar to that which I observed among the Wovan. Noting a Gebusi informant's statement, "If I had a sister, then, I would marry but since I don't, I'll just stay as is" (Knauft 1985:169), Knauft draws attention to public ideology. The cross-sibling relationship is characterized by interdependency in that each sibling figures prominently in the possible marital career of the other. However, the Gebusi, like the Arapesh, Bun, and Wovan, are not stymied by a simple failure of demographics to provide appropriate exchange partners. "In cases where demography and kinship preclude even a diffuse intention of reciprocity, a payment of foods is sometimes made to the wife-givers. This one-time payment is not obligatory and is relatively small" (Knauft 1985:170).

Gebusi parallels with the Wovan situation run even deeper, however, in that the best laid plans of Gebusi men go oft aglee at the hands of "wild women," to use Sharon Tiffany's phrase (1985). "Romantic sexual attraction is believed to be the cause of many or most nonreciprocal marriages and may in fact thwart sister exchanges that have been planned" (Knauft 1985:172). The issue is not whether such marriages occur, they undoubtedly do, but how they are conceptualized to conform ultimately to the public ideology. "The cross-cutting features of romantic, reciprocated, and nonreciprocated marriages provide affinal flexibility and allow demographic realities and personal preferences to be accommodated" (Knauft 1985:175).

This very brief excursion into fringe Highlands' ethnography is intended merely to make clear that any account of marrying as social action, whether it be through brother/sister exchange or by some alternative means, must take into account that indigenous constructions of indigenous practice are themselves central aspects of the systems we are trying to explain and cannot merely be dismissed as anomalous.

## Santa Cruz

Shifting to my comparative frame, we find in "East Bay" that "marriage is as much a kind of political affair between sets of kin as it is the means by which a new household is established" (Davenport 1965:172). While Wovan restrict the decision-making power of any young man in relation to arranged marriage, Lenidu (the inhabitants of Santa Cruz) exclude both males and females. "When it is time for them to be married, young single adults are never consulted. They are not even permitted to express their wishes about marriage until negotiations are well under way" (Davenport 1965:172). However, just as we found among Wovan women, ultimate control over marital careers rests with the parties themselves. "If for some reason either of the betrothed flatly refuses to marry the other, the whole affair may be called off" (Davenport 1965:173). Unlike Wovan, however, Lenidu youths, both male and female, appear much more tractable and more accepting of their parents' wishes. "Young adults seem always to feel that their parents are the best judges of a spouse for them, in so far as considerations of morality, ability to bear children, and willingness to work are concerned. Parents, on the other hand, believe that their children are the only judges as to whether or not the spouse selected will be physically and sexually attractive" (1965:173).

In his paper "Social Structure of Santa Cruz Island" (1964), Davenport outlines his major concerns with Santa Cruz social organization. The complexity of the system compared to our New Guinea Highlands examples is immediately apparent. Exchange networks between islands in which women, wives, and concubines flow in one direction, while red feather money flows in the counter direction make up the total system. Relatedness is still manipulable—adoption is of major significance in the lives of a large percentage of the people (1964: 69)—but membership in descent groups is fixed at birth.

Unlike the Wovan who strive to maintain a semblance of equality in all things, for Lenidu long-lasting indebtedness creates the hierarchical relations between men. "Marriage is considered to be made possible by the men who contribute toward the groom's bride-price, and only by them" (Davenport 1964:72). The extended family is a hierarchically structured institution with the relations between its constituent men immutable.

> From the point of view of anyone in the extended family, the group should always act in cooperative unison under the direction of its senior man. To a subordinate member, the authority this senior man exerts is unsurpassed by any other authority or relationship. A second pattern of important authority relations in this society has to do with the authority of men over women, and in particular of a brother over his sister and of a husband over his wife. A brother always has economic and jural interests in his sister even after her marriage, and she is obliged to assist him occasionally with matters pertaining to his (and her natal) extended family. (Davenport 1964:73–74)

Here, too, however, the problematic of cross-sex siblingship and marriage is apparent. The relationship between a man and his sister continues after her marriage and can be the source of tension between a man and his sister's husband. Because a woman's relationships to her husband and her brother are very similar, "this makes the jural relationship between a wife's brother and his [sic] sister's husband complex and delicate; a relationship where conflicts of interest easily develop" (Davenport 1964:74).

Davenport continues his exploration of Santa Cruz social structure in much greater detail in a series of papers in the *Baessler-Archiv, Beitrage zur volkerkunde,* in 1968, 1969, and 1972. In most cases marriages are accompanied by substantial brideprice payments (1968a:168–69; 1968b:237–38; 1969:191; 1972:36–39). While the bride's father is heavily involved in negotiations and in the receipt and distribution of bridewealth, there is always an element of choice and personal attraction in the final arrangements. Rules, as we have seen before, are more involved in establishing what one cannot do, such as marrying one's "actual parallel cousin" (1972:35), or what is considered "merely inappropriate" (1968a:167) rather than in prescribing what one must do.

Rules and actions, structure and sentiment must necessarily be accounted for in any attempt to understand the cultural construction of kinship relationships. In "Kinship and Sentiment in Santa Cruz" (1976), Davenport provides his initial formulation of this problem. "What is real to a person of Santa Cruz (Lenidu) is the sentiment or affective component of kinship relations" (1976:1). Kinship behavior, etiquette is a compound of respect, and shame.

> While descent is fixed inalterably at birth, filiation, that is kinship, is not so rigidly determined. Fosterage, which until recently altered the parental status of 30% of all children, does change kin relations. Ritual kinship also alters kin relationships for a few adults. As important as fosterage is the fact that so-called classificatory relatives often replace or usurp the prime positions of the principal, or central kin types of a kinship category. Even in the case of primary relatives, such as a *tute-* (F), a classificatory *tute-* may take over or replace the status and role of the real, or genealogically specified 'father.' Of course, such replacement occurs when the prime or central kinsman/woman dies, but more important are occasions when this occurs as part of the politics of kinship. (Davenport 1976:4)

While kin are expected to behave toward one another as friends, one needs another kind of construction to seek friendship without kinship connection. "Traditionally, all kin are in terms of sentiment some kind of 'friend.' The bond of friend without kinship is a special status/role, called *odu*, which in English is better described as 'ritual friend.' It is the most intense interpersonal relationship in Nidu society" (Davenport 1976:4).

Returning to our concern with hierarchy and equality, and again in contrast to the Wovan situation in which even genealogically structured relationships of inequality are ritually reconstructed into egalitarian "partnerships,"

> all status/role relationships [in Santa Cruz] are conceived of as either indebted, uneven and complementary *(tao)* or equal, egalitarian, or symmetric *(tuku tao)*. Close or effective kin relations are either one or the other, *tao* or *tuku tao*, and cannot be altered except by degrees of *tao*. Distant kin, friendships and non-kin relations are *tuku tao* until an individual gives support of either the *okati* or *atwaoda* sort. The relation becomes *tao*. If the support were classed as *okati*, then the relation remains fixedly complementary. If the support were classed as *atwaoda*, the relation is *tao* until the obligation is discharged. When discharged the relationship becomes *atulwa*, and again symmetric. (Davenport 1976:5)

"Both the symmetry and complementarity of kin relationships can never be changed. Therefore, the concept of *atulwa*, because it follows from *atwaoda*, is not applicable to close or effective kinship" (Davenport 1976:5). (*Okati* and *atwaoda* are glossed as social support and social investment—the latter being given by non-kin, never by even distant kin, with an expectation of a return, the former being given by distant-kin, never non-kin, and including moral support and support in arms, and being given with no expectation of a return except in kind.)

What are the lessons of the Santa Cruz case? First, despite the major differences we see in surface phenomena, it is necessary to recognize that at deeper levels we are dealing with a limited set of "cultural counters." Concern with hierarchy and equality, concern with the relationship between cross-sex siblings, concern with the relationship between husbands and wives, and more generally between men and women, may manifest themselves differently and may be given alternative solutions in the two ethnographic settings but the underlying concerns remain the same.

More importantly, Davenport has drawn attention to the necessity of understanding sentiment if we are to understand kinship.

## Commentary

Despite the considerable ethnographic literature on the importance of siblingship in Pacific social organization in general (Marshall 1983) and New Guinea social organization in particular (Kelly 1977), it appears we continue to divorce (no pun intended) the discussion of marriage, including so-called sister exchange marriage or, to use a less androcentric term, brother/sister exchange marriage, from the discussion of siblingship.

In 1916, Thurnwald drew the distinction between those societies in which "women were bought" and those in which wives were obtained by "mutual exchange" (1916:274). He went further to suggest (as indeed we now see with the Wovan, Bun, and Arapesh and Gebusi) that if "mutual exchange cannot take place, on account of lack of women, objects of value are made to substitute to make good the balance" among the Banaro (1916:274). Since the publication of Collier and Rosaldo's "Politics and Gender in Simple Societies" (1981), the division of societies into those with brideservice and those with sister exchange has remained a subject of debate.

If I may again quote Knauft at some length on this issue, "The lack of brideservice among the Gebusi is particularly striking because they fit so many of the characteristics that Collier and Rosaldo (1981) posit as central to 'brideservice societies.' Among these are an egalitarian political structure among adult men, a lack of bridewealth or strong valuation of material wealth objects, a hunting/gathering horticultural mode of subsistence, lack of effective controls over ultimate violence, and a male status system in which the attainment of marriage is central" (1985:411n. 17).

Tuzin (1976) similarly suggests that "if all marriages were counted in which the *spirit* of exchange was the guiding principle the total would certainly exceed 50 percent" among the Ilahita Arapesh (1976:103–04).

Woodburn discusses situations, very similar to those experienced by Knauft and myself, of noncompetitive egalitarianism in contrast to situations in which equality is asserted through competitive transactions (Woodburn 1982; see also Flanagan 1989; Strathern 1985).

It may be asked, as Knauft does, whether brideservice per se is as necessary and central to the articulation of politics in simple societies as is implied by labeling them "brideservice societies" (1985:411).

We need to be aware of the extent to which our language in exchange systems may bias our perceptions. Laurel Bossen (1988) has proposed a critical reexamination of the anthropological terminology of marriage transactions. Arguing that anthropology has perceived men as transactors and women as transacted, she calls for an examination of the way in which women compete for the economic services of men (Flanagan 1989:252).

Luce Irigaray criticizes Levi-Straussean models of the circulation of women on the basis of their androcentric biases. "Woman," Irigaray says, "exists only as an occasion for mediation, transaction, transition, transference, between man and his fellow man, indeed between man and himself" (1985:193; see Flanagan 1989:252).

Wovan men, like men everywhere, find women problematic and their behavior disconcerting. Men construct models of the universe in which women are subservient and obedient. But enforcing these models, in terms of social action, would immeasurably impoverish their own experience (Flanagan 1988b:15–16). Despite the claims of Wovan men, the freedom of young women is not detrimental to their experience or to Wovan cultural continuity. Rather it is integral to it. As Roy Wagner has phrased it, "the final arbiter of accuracy in social relations is meaning and point of view rather than externally construed material result" (1988:49). In Wovan, it is through the dynamic of "failed" exchange that women and men continue to define themselves for themselves and for each other.

## References Cited

Bradburd, Daniel. 1984. "The Rules and the Game: The Practice of Marriage Among the Komachi." *American Ethnologist* 11(4): 738–53

Chowning, A., and W.H. Goodenough. 1971. "Lakalai Political Organization." In *Politics in New Guinea*, ed. Ronald Berndt and Peter Lawrence, pp. 113–74. Nedlands: University of Western Australia Press.

Collier, Jane F., and Michelle Z. Rosaldo. 1981. "Politics and Gender in Simple Societies." In *Sexual Meanings*, ed. Sherry Ortner and Harriet Whitehead, pp. 275–330. Cambridge: The University Press.

Comrie, Bernard. 1987. "Grammatical Relations, Semantic Roles and Topic-comment Structure in a New Guinea Highland Language: Harway." In *Language Topics*, ed. Ross Steele and Terry Threadgold, pp. 355–66. Amsterdam: John Benjamins.

Davenport, William H. 1960. *Jamaican Fishing: A Game Theory*

*Analysis*. Yale University Publications in Anthropology, No. 59, New Haven.

———. 1964. "Social Structure of Santa Cruz Island." In *Explorations in Cultural Anthropology*, ed. W.H. Goodenough, pp. 57–93. New York: McGraw-Hill.

———. 1965. "Sexual Patterns and Their Regulation in a Society of the Southwest Pacific." In *Sex and Behavior*, ed. F. Beach, pp. 164–207. New York: Wiley.

———. 1968a. "Social Organization Notes on the Northern Santa Cruz Islands: The Duff Islands (Taumako)." *Baessler-Archiv*, n.f., 16:137–205.

———. 1968b. "Social Organization Notes on the Southern Santa Cruz Islands: Utupua and Vanikoro." *Baessler-Archiv*, n.f., 16:207–75.

———. 1969. "Social Organization Notes on the Northern Santa Cruz Islands: The Main Reef Islands." *Baessler-Archiv*, n.f., 17:151–243.

———. 1972. "Social Organization Notes on the Northern Santa Cruz Islands: The Outer Reef Islands." *Baessler-Archiv*, n.f., 20:11–95.

———. 1976. "Kinship and Sentiment in Santa Cruz Island Society." Seminar paper, Anthropology Department, University of Pennsylvania.

Flanagan, J.G. 1988a. "The Cultural Construction of Equality on the New Guinea Highlands' Fringe." In *Rules, Decisions, and Inequality in Egalitarian Societies*, ed. James G. Flanagan and Steve Rayner, pp. 166–80. Brookfield, Vt.: Gower.

———. 1988b. "Right of Refusal: Women and Disorder in Papua New Guinea." Paper presented at the Annual Meetings of the American Ethnological Association, St. Louis, Missouri.

———. 1989. "Hierarchy in Simple 'Egalitarian' Societies." *Annual Review of Anthropology* 18:245–66.

Goodenough, Ward H., ed. 1964. *Explorations in Cultural Anthropology*. New York: McGraw Hill.

Irigaray, L. 1985. *This sex which is not One*. Trans. Catherine Porter. Ithaca, N.Y.: Cornell University Press.

Kelly, Raymond. 1977. *Etoro Social Structure*. Ann Arbor: Michigan University Press.

Knauft, Bruce. 1985. *Good Company and Violence*. Berkeley: University of California Press.

Lambert, Bernd. 1983. "Equivalence, Authority, and Complementarity in Butaritari-Makin Sibling Relations." In *Siblingship in Oceania*, ed. Mac Marshall, pp. 149–200. ASAO Monograph No. 8. New York: University Press of America.

Marshall, Mac, ed. 1983. *Siblingship in Oceania*. ASAO Monograph No. 8. New York: University Press of America.

McDowell, N. 1990. "Causing an Uproar: Women's Marital Strategies in So-called Sister Exchange." Paper presented at the Annual Meeting of the American Anthropological Association, New Orleans.

Mead, G.H. 1934. *Mind, Self and Society*. Chicago: University of Chicago Press.

Saul, Mahir. 1989. "Corporate Authority, Exchange, and Personal Opposition in Bobo Marriages." *American Ethnologist* 16(1): 57–74.

Schneider, David. 1992. "Ethnocentrism and the Notion of Kinship." *Man* 27(3): 629–31.

Strathern, Marilyn. 1985. "Kinship and Economy: Constitutive Orders of a Provisional Kind." *American Ethnologist* 12(2): 191–209.

Thurnwald, Richard. 1916. *Banaro Society*. Memoirs of the American Anthropological Association, Vol. 3, No. 4. Lancaster, Pa.

Tiffany, Sharon. 1985. *The Wild Woman*. Cambridge, Mass.: Schenkman.

Tuzin, Donald. 1976. *The Ilahita Arapesh*. Berkeley: University of California Press.

Wagner, Roy. 1988. "Visible Sociality: The Daribi Community." In *Mountain Papuans*, ed. James F. Weiner, pp. 39–72. Ann Arbor: University of Michigan Press.

Watson, James B. 1970. "Society as Organized Flow: The Atirora Case." *South Western Journal of Anthropology* 26:107–24.

# Kinship and Social Organization: Traditional Issues in the Study of Modernity

*William W. Donner*

The study of kinship and social organization was central in the writing and teaching of many of my teachers, including Bill Davenport. Although these topics were central to anthropology when I was a graduate student in the 1970s, they no longer seem to be very important in contemporary anthropology: they are no longer topics of a self-conscious or explicit academic discourse and they have lost much of their centrality in anthropological thinking over the past twenty years. I will begin this paper by exploring why kinship and social organization have lost their centrality in anthropology. Then I will propose that anthropologists broaden their perspectives to re-examine not only kinship but also broader issues concerning social differentiation, integration, and community organization in modernizing social systems. Throughout the paper, I will suggest that anthropologists should reconsider some traditional issues in the study of kinship and social organization before—as Bill recently put it—we forget what we have learned and are forced to rediscover them all over again.

For the purposes of this paper, I will consider social organization to be the study of social relations, roles, groups, and categories.[1] Kinship is study of the social groups, relations, and the culturally determined constructions, metaphors, interpretations, and meanings that are derived from biological reproduction. Kinship, thus, includes the study of groups, relations, and also cultural understandings about groups and relations. In small-scale communities, such as Sikaiana where I did fieldwork, important social relations are based upon kinship. As small-scale communities have become involved in a global system, new non-kinship roles and institutions have become important in forming groups and relations. Many of these new institutions and roles articulate local communities with larger social systems at the same time that they differentiate groups and relations within these communities.

## The Marginalization of Kinship and Social Organization

Defining academic interests is always a perilous task. But it seems clear that over the past twenty years, the study of kinship and social organization has lost two essential features of importance in academic discussion: reflexivity and centrality.

Certain academic issues involve a high degree of reflexivity and self-consciousness, especially in defining terms and concepts. Such, for example, was the case in kinship studies through the 1960s when definitions of "marriage," "descent," "lineage," "alliance," "structure," and even "kinship" itself were debated. This kind of reflexivity no longer exists in kinship studies, although many can argue with justification that everyone is much the better for it.

Some academic topics are central in the sense that a discipline is especially concerned with them or other topics are dependent upon them. Math has a high degree of centrality, underpinning engineering, statistics, physics, and other quantitative fields. English, in so far as it concerns writing, also seems to have a high degree of centrality at least within an undergraduate college curriculum. The analysis of social groups and relations, especially those based upon kinship, has lost this kind of centrality over the past twenty years.

In anthropology, the explicit concern with groups and relations is often associated with British social anthropology. Social anthropologists analyzed groups and relations, especially kinship-based ones, as interrelated "social facts" (Durkheim 1933, 1951; Radcliffe-Brown 1952). There were other approaches to the study of kinship which took a more mentalistic perspective, including approaches which can be termed cognitive (Goodenough 1970; Scheffler and Lounsbury 1971), structural (Levi-Strauss 1969), and symbolic (Schneider 1968). By the 1960s, social anthropologists were developing approaches which examined individual choices and changes in the formation of groups and relations, an approach which would come to be known as "processual" (Barth 1966; Leach 1954; Turner 1957). Although the study of groups and relations was never quite as central for most American anthropologists as it was for their British counterparts, it did have a centrality which was reflected in the writing of important American anthropologists (Morgan 1870; Kroeber 1909; Lowie 1948; Murdock 1949; Goodenough 1970).

There are numerous examples of the marginalization of kinship and social organization in anthropological discourse and thinking. There are very few job openings which seek a specialty in kinship and social organization. In the December 1993 *Anthropology Newsletter*, for example, I counted the specializations listed in 35 advertisements for social-cultural anthropologists. Social organization was listed in two openings (one was a temporary position). It was behind ethnic and/or cultural identity (5), political economy (5), urban anthropology (6), applied anthropology (5), environment and ecology (5). (I did not count area specialties or specialties concerning specific social groups such as African-Americans, Asian-Americans, women.) When I was a graduate student at the University of Pennsylvania, a graduate course in social organization was taught every year, one of three courses from the cultural quadrant required for all graduate students. It is now taught occasionally as an optional course.

If one wanted to teach an undergraduate course in kinship and social organization, I don't know of any current textbook for the subject, whereas twenty years ago there would have been a wide selection. Many of the texts are out of print, for example, Pasternak (1976), Graburn (1971), Bohannon and Middleton (1968). Fox (1967) and Keesing (1975) are still in print but essentially unchanged in twenty years, although one could argue that nothing much has happened in the study of kinship for over twenty years. The publication dates of these textbooks correspond with the high degree of centrality of kinship and social organization in the late 1960s and early 1970s (Barnes 1971; Fortes 1969; Kuper 1972; Goodenough 1970; Needham 1971; Goody 1973). But by the early 1980s, even the people who had been leading writers about kinship and social organization were questioning the utility of these studies (see Schneider 1984; Kuper 1982).

The *Biennial Review of Anthropology* always had an article devoted to social organization. When it became the *Annual Review of Anthropology* in 1972, social organization was dropped as a permanent topic. The indexes in the current *Annual Review of Anthropology* do not list social organization as a subheading. The closest subheading is "political and social relations."

In January 1994, I checked the Social Science Index citation list for references in three journals which I consider to be central in anthropological thinking: *Man, American Ethnologist* and *American Anthropologist*. In these three journals there were a total of 7068 references for the ten years from February 1983 through November 24, 1993. "Social organization" as a topic pulled only 39 references across all three journals. "Kinship" did better with 171. "Family" had 106. "Descent," a central concept when I was learning social organization in the 1970s, received a total of 7. The term "lineage(s)" appeared in 11 citations (one of which was by me). I confess to undergoing some marginalization myself, so I am not certain about the most important terms in contemporary anthropology. Searching for terms which might reflect current anthropological interests, I found the topic of "Women" received 250; "gender" as a topic pulled 133 articles. "Power," apparently hotter than anything except "women," had 190 citations attached to it. "Social organization" by these standards is quite marginalized. "Descent," a central concept at mid-century (Goodenough 1955; Davenport 1959, 1963; Fortes 1969), is a non-topic (see Kuper 1982). "Family" and "Kinship," although important, are no longer central.[2]

The vitality of an academic subject can be questioned when there are no longer articles and textbooks about it, graduate courses in it, or advertised jobs calling for expertise in it.

Kinship and social organization are not completely forgotten. They are implicit topics in many papers, including many of the articles in the *Annual Review*. Obviously, the papers in this book express a strong interest in kinship relations. Most introductory textbooks continue to devote several chapters to kinship, including discussions of classic issues such as kinship classification systems and descent systems. Many studies that are primarily oriented to the topic of gender, or more specifically to an emphasis on the study of women's roles and behavior, are clearly concerned with the core issues of kinship and social organization (see, for example, Collier and Yanagisako 1987). But the vibrancy of these gender studies has not been incorporated into new understandings of kinship and social organization. Instead, these more recent studies of women's roles seem to be incorporated into discussions about power relations, ideologies, and gender roles, both of the observed and the observing anthropologists themselves.

Traditional concerns of social organization are an implicit issue in another discussion of high centrality—various theories of agency or action (see Ortner 1984). Indeed, the flaws in older concepts of "social structure" provided the impetus for early discussions of processes and action. But again these theories of action seem to have a direction of their own and are not directly oriented to the issues examined in earlier discussions of kinship, groups, or relations.

## Things Change

I can think of many reasons why kinship and social organization have lost their centrality. First, things change. I think it was Margaret Mead who noted that when she started fieldwork every monograph had a section devoted to what was done with umbilical cords after childbirth. Over the course of her career, anthropologists lost interest in umbilical cords. As an undergraduate student I had to read Kroeber and Wissler's work on culture areas in North America; I would not be surprised if not a single anthropology student has opened those books in fifteen years, unless by mistake. When I was a graduate student in the late 1970s, the evolutionary theories of White, Steward, Sahlins, and Service, and materialist approaches generally, had to be taken seriously, although they too have been marginalized (Murphy 1978). As a graduate student, I used the Human Relations Area Files. Although these may never have been very central to anthropological theory, I judge them to be far more peripheral now than twenty-five years ago when Murdock was writing. As an undergraduate student, I read about people who gave Rorschach tests to determine personality traits in different cultures. I assume such studies are no longer conducted, or at least they have become quite rare. As a graduate student, I was assured by very distinguished visiting speakers that Claude Levi-Strauss had developed an essential theory for understanding human thought. I would say that over the past fifteen years, the "master" (as one speaker described him) has undergone considerable marginalization (as has this speaker himself). Structuralism, culture and personality, kinship and social organization, all seem to have gone the way of the umbilical cord.

There are other important reasons besides changing fashion for the marginalization of kinship and social organization. Many studies in social organization relied upon conceptualizing a "structure," a pattern of relations or statuses which was simultaneously abstract and concrete. Relations were distilled to these abstract structures which were given misleading connotations of concreteness. Individual agency was often ignored in the concern for constructing these abstract structures. Studies of groups and relations, moreover, rarely concerned themselves with emotions and feelings, as if stripping relations of emotion made the project more concrete. But emotions are at the core of kinship relations (see Davenport 1976). Lack of attention to emotion and agency was a longstanding fault of approaches as different as those of structural-functionalism (Radcliffe-Brown 1952; Fortes 1969), cognitive approaches (Kroeber 1909; Goodenough 1965, 1970; Scheffler and Lounsbury 1971), and structuralists (Levi-Strauss 1969; Needham 1962). The structural-functionalists reduced kinship to jural relations, the cognitive anthropologists to semantic distinctive features, and the structuralists to basic logical constructs of human thought.

By the early 1970s, kinship and social organization also suffered from the very fact that they had a high degree of theoretical centrality. Because they were central to anthropological theory for so long, discourses about kinship and social organization had accumulated everything that was faulty in anthropological thinking, notably the lack of concern with change, history, and agency, and the bias towards focusing on male activities. Areas of specialization in anthropology which developed more recently (for example, medical anthropology, ethnolinguistics, or anthropology and education) were not as hampered by these deficiencies and as they developed they included broader understandings of human behavior.

Moreover, being so central to anthropology for so long, kinship and social organization also suffered from being the topics of long-standing and convoluted debates. The very fact of their reflexivity and centrality made them extremely cumbersome topics by the 1970s. There were endless petty debates in which different writers either misunderstood or misrepresented their opponents in presenting their own arguments. One of the more notorious debates centered around "alliance" theories of marriage (Levi-Strauss 1969). Over the course of twenty years, Homans and Schneider (1955) challenged Levi-Strauss (1969; originally published in 1949); they were challenged by Needham (1962) in defense of Levi-Strauss; and Needham was himself criticized by Levi-Strauss in the introduction of the English translation of Levi-Strauss's book, which Needham himself edited. Such controversies, and there seemed to be many of them, bored many of the graduate students I knew, especially since we found the writing of many of those involved to be opaque.

People writing about social organization felt obliged to define concepts such as "clan," "lineage," "descent," "marriage," "family," and "household." The definitions were often broad and tortured in their attempts to be both universal and useful: they never seemed adequate for understanding the unique conditions in specific societies. Writing papers about kinship required reviewing these debates, and tortuously trying to sort out each critic's (mis)interpretations of their predecessor. I suspect that for many people it seemed much easier to simply start all over again with new topics, such as "agent," "power" or "women." Like troublesome cars which are easier to junk than fix, many anthropologists found it easier to abandon studying kinship and social organization rather than try to fix them.

There were other problems with the study of kinship and social organization which derived from both the changing conditions of anthropology and the world. Until fairly recently, many anthropologists presented studies of isolated and in some sense changeless people, detached from time and place. Too many anthropologists overemphasized the "timeless" internal dynamics of the communities they studied and minimized the manner in which tribal and village societies were being pulled into a world system. Nevertheless, there were some cases in the early 20th century, for example in the relatively small-scale societies of Oceania, where I think anthropologists could legitimately claim that they were studying tribal and village communities that were in an important sense "kinship based." By the 1970s and 1980s, the illusion of isolation was no longer tenable. People living in the most isolated societies were radically changed by their incorporation into global social-economic systems (Wallerstein 1979; Chirot and Hall 1982; Featherstone 1990; Hannerz 1992; Foster 1991). People work for wages in new occupations with specialized expertise, they migrate to urban centers where they assume new ethnic identities and occupations, and they interact in many relations other than those based upon kinship.

At about the same time that anthropologists recognized the differentiation of local communities, anthropology as a discipline also differentiated. New kinds of anthropologists emerged who focused their research on specialized topics: economics, politics, medicine, language use, education, food, ethnicity, gender, even "consciousness," among many others. While there is no journal or professional organization devoted to the study of kinship and social organization, there are journals, many started in the last twenty years, devoted to these more recently developed topics. With the many subsections, associations, and councils in the American Anthropological Association, there is no section on family, kinship, and social organization. I suspect this lack of institutionalized interest came about because the centrality of kinship and social organization was assumed at the time when anthropology began to differentiate. As anthropologists specialized into various new subfields, new journals and associations were developed to reflect these new specializations. But instead of continuing, this old core of anthropology fragmented and disintegrated.[3]

## Who Cares?

There are several reasons why I think the topic of kinship deserves both more centrality and reflexivity. First, American society is rife with debates about the "family," debates which concern many issues central in the study of kinship. In this debate anthropologists are strangely quiet. Students reading introductory texts ask me questions reflecting the limitations of the texts' definitions of kinship relations. These definitions are inadequate to handle the complex range of kinship relations in the United States which includes male homosexual marriages, single parent households, unmarried mothers, incest, and family abuse. These topics are part of a highly reflexive and central national debate.[4]

Second, kinship relations remain important in the lives of the people about whom anthropologists write. In my own field research on Sikaiana in the Solomon Islands, I found many important changes derived from the introduction of Western roles and institutions. Nevertheless, kinship-based relations remain quite important. Sikaiana lineages still hold shared rights to important economic resources and also figure prominently in exchange relations. There are very high rates of fosterage (in the 1980s about 50% of the children on Sikaiana were residing with their foster parents; this figure was lower, about 25%, for migrants in towns). Households, both on Sikaiana and among migrants in Honiara, are based upon extended kinship ties. Some traditional prohibitions on interaction between certain relatives, especially prohibitions on behavior between opposite-sex in-laws and opposite-sex siblings, are still followed by many people.

For me, then, there are two good reasons to be concerned with the study of kinship: it is important in our own lives and it is important in the lives of the people we write about.

## Differentiation and Integration

As discussed above, the organization of groups and relations changes as small-scale communities become involved in larger regional and international systems. The present-day study of social groups and relations must examine how kinship-based relations become less encompassing, and new roles, institutions, and groups are introduced or developed. Many of these changes result from the internal differentiation of local social groups and relations and the integration of these local relations and groups into larger regional and ultimately global systems and processes.

These processes of integration and differentiation are evident on Sikaiana, an atoll about 100 miles east of Malaita Island in the Solomon Islands. Sikaiana is inhabited by about 200–250 people who are Polynesian in their cultural traditions. Before contact with Europeans in the 19th century, Sikaiana was quite isolated. With the exception of occasional migrants who traveled long distances in canoes, everyone on the atoll was biologically related. The major social groups, including land-owning lineages, chiefly and commoner clans, and households, were all kinship based. As discussed above, significant social relations on Sikaiana are still based upon kinship. There are, however, many new kinds of groups and relations, mostly introduced and developed in the past sixty years, which are not kinship based and result from Sikaiana's integration into a world system.

During the 19th century, Sikaiana had fairly frequent contacts with whalers and traders and was one of the popular stops for Europeans in the Solomon Islands. In the 1890s, Sikaiana was nominally incorporated into the British Solomon Islands Protectorate. By 1900, trade goods including cloth, steel tools and utensils, and tobacco were important in the local economy. During the early part of this century, Sikaiana men were eager to work for wages, often as crewmen on government ships. In the 1930s, the atoll's population rapidly converted to Christianity. Following World War II, the government established many Western institutions in Sikaiana, including a court, a council, a primary school (which it took over from the Melanesian Mission), a cooperative store, and a medical clinic. Moreover, the total population tripled in this century. Although the population residing on Sikaiana has remained relatively stable at about 200–250 people, there has been permanent migration to other parts of the Solomon Islands, in particular Honiara, the nation's capital.

Some of the changes in Sikaiana social relations can be described in terms of their increased specialization and differentiation. New kinds of relations have been developed which presume specialized expertise derived from global institutions. On the atoll, these include priests, catechists, teachers, court justices, local government representatives, and committee members. Most Sikaiana are involved in these roles, and the institutions associated with these roles are integral in Sikaiana life. Moreover, migrants who live in Honiara are involved in wage labor and a market-based economy. They work in specialized occupations and professions—as laborers, carpenters, administrators, teachers, nurses, professionals—and in businesses. The integration of the Sikaiana people into a regional and international social system is part of the same process in which there is some internal differentiation of social relations within the community. A Sikaiana electrician performs occupational tasks very similar to electricians everywhere in the world, but these tasks require knowledge which is unknown to many other Sikaiana.

Similar issues of differentiation and integration and how they are associated with migration, urbanization, capitalism, and industrialization were central to the founding thinkers of social theory. They often used ideal types to compare relationships in societies of different scale: Gemeinschaft/Gesellschaft (Tonnies 1957), "mechanical/organic solidarity" (Durkheim 1933), "traditional/rational-bureaucratic" (Weber 1947), "primary/secondary" (Cooley 1923, chapters 3 and 4; Park 1915), "folk/urban" (Redfield 1947), "uniplex/multiplex" (Gluckman 1955, 1962), and "diffuse/specific," "particularistic/universalistic," "ascribed/achieved," "affective/affective neutrality" (Parsons 1951, 1966; Parsons and Shils 1951; see summaries by Stein 1960; Benedict 1968; Miner 1952, 1968; Berreman 1978).

These approaches were never very central in anthropological thinking. Anthropologists were never happy with the tendency to examine these processes of change in terms of an opposition between "traditional" and "modern" (see, for example, Geertz 1963). Anthropologists argued that the so-called traditional societies were quite variable, as are the routes to becoming "modern." Anthropologists, moreover, found "modern" to be an ethnocentric term, often being described in terms of

Western values and assumptions, and presuming a kind of progressivism.

These traditional concerns of social theory may be more relevant to anthropology than is currently appreciated because 19th and early 20th century social theorists witnessed the breakdown of village and community social systems, migration, the shift from a craft to market economy. These are changes affecting many contemporary small-scale societies such as Sikaiana.

In a recent examination of how modernity affects social relations and local social systems, Giddens (1990, 1991) argues that time and space become disrupted from their local context and "disembedded" into a global system. Time on Sikaiana, for example, is measured by Western standards, especially those of the church calendar with its yearly holidays and weekly events such as communion on Wednesdays and Sundays. Daily routine is structured around church services, one in the morning and another in the evening. Space is disembedded by the constant circular migration of Sikaiana people between Sikaiana and Honiara, and by the media. Most Sikaiana have a radio and some follow world events with interest, often telling me what was happening in the United States. Giddens also argues that local symbols of interaction become replaced by universal tokens. Cash replaces reciprocity as the basis for exchange. A Sikaiana person must now earn money to purchase the necessities of life. On Sikaiana these necessities include steel tools, cooking utensils, kerosene, and clothing. Most migrants living in Honiara are totally dependent on cash to pay rent, buy food and necessities.

Although Gidden's concepts explain important features of present-day Sikaiana life, the disembedding is far from complete. There are still local measures of time based upon wind direction, constellations, and seasons for various fish. Sikaiana people still prefer to live near each other when they migrate to other parts of the Solomon Islands. The Sikaiana also have maintained and developed new exchange activities which are not determined by markets and are similar to those which Mauss (1990) described as total prestations. These include marriage exchanges, competitive exchanges centering around children, and more informal but still very important patterns of generalized reciprocity.

## Modernity, Self and Community

Based upon their observations of Western societies, some sociologists have often associated social differentiation and modernity with increased individualism (Durkheim 1933; Weber 1976; Simmel 1950, 1971). Writing from this general perspective, Giddens (1990, 1991) argues that in modernizing societies the self becomes detached from communal and ascribed relations, notably those associated with kinship, and becomes developed by personal choices and experiences. The self becomes a life-long project which is constructed and reconstructed out of choices and intimate relations. Modernity also presumes not only a heightened sense of self but also a heightened sense of self-consciousness. Indeed, many argue that self-consciousness is a distinctive trait of modernity.[5]

I found it difficult to examine this issue on Sikaiana because I cannot determine how Sikaiana people talked about the self before intensive contact with Europeans. In their language, daily speech and gossip, they are highly aware of motivations and analytical about behavior. The large number of words describing these behaviors suggests that the Sikaiana were very astute and reflexive observers of motivations and intentions long before they had any contact with Europeans. But I did not find Sikaiana people to be highly introspective or self-reflective about their own lives, especially by the middle-class, Western standards outlined by Giddens.

I did, however, find an area of their social life in which the Sikaiana are constantly redefining their social relations in a highly self-conscious and introspective manner. This area concerns their communal activities. Although they are not especially self-conscious about their own selves as life projects, they are highly self-conscious about their community and the changes that it has undergone. Moreover, during my fieldwork in the 1980s, many Sikaiana were self-consciously trying to develop and maintain their communal organizations. Some of this self-consciousness is found in their discussions about *kastom* (from English "custom"), their customary or traditional practices (see Donner 1992, 1993; Keesing and Tonkinson 1982; Jolly and Thomas 1992; Lindstrom and White 1993).

There are several very explicit efforts to maintain their community identity. Early in my first stay in 1980, the Sikaiana people held a meeting to try to find support for a resettlement community. Because of the increase in their population, many Sikaiana people are forced to migrate away from the atoll. Although the idea for the resettlement community was motivated by the desire for land, it was also motivated by the desire to find an area where they could live together to maintain their traditions. Outside of Honiara, about 20 Sikaiana families have bought land near the Tenaru River where they form a suburban ethnic community.

The Sikaiana have found other ways to distinguish themselves from other Solomon Islanders and develop distinctive cultural practices amongst themselves. In their song composition, younger people began to play guitars with Western tunes but they composed songs in the Sikaiana language about Sikaiana themes and events. Although many young men prefer to hold informal conversations in the lingua franca of the Solomon Islands, Pijin, and Pijin would give them access to a much larger audience which includes other Solomon Islanders, they continue to compose songs in the Sikaiana vernacular, limiting their audience to other Sikaiana people (Donner 1987, 1992). Sikaiana have formed a number of committees which are directly concerned with their welfare. Following a cyclone in 1986, the Sikaiana inhabitants of Honiara formed a committee and held fundraising events to collect money for people on Sikaiana. In 1987, Sikaiana migrants formed a sports association to encourage the rehearsals of traditional dances and organize Sikaiana participation in Honiara sports leagues. During my stay in 1987, most Sikaiana residing in Honiara participated in this association's activities (see Donner 1992, 1993). In the early 1990s, there were continual activities to raise money for a church which was built at the Sikaiana settlement at Tenaru.

Thus in many respects, the entire community—not the self—is a continuing project with a high degree of reflexivity. The construction of this community takes place in the context of powerful forces for internal differentiation within the community and the integration of the community into a world system of economic, political and cultural relations. The Sikaiana emphasis upon constructing local identities and meanings is a form of differentiation which has parallels in many other small-scale communities as they come under pressure to blend into a larger global and cultural system (Appadurai 1990; Thomas 1992; Foster 1991). These constructions of local identities are not so much the revival of traditional culture as the reconstruction of distinctive collective identities in the context of a modern global system (see, for example, Robertson 1992).

## Conclusion: Contemporary Issues in Social Organization

A variety of forces negatively affected interest in the study of kinship and social organization. Studies of kinship and social organization were overly abstract, static, and devoid of emotion and change. Because they developed near the center of anthropological theory during the first three quarters of the 20th century, approaches to kinship and social organization contained and reflected the biases and deficiencies of that anthropology. For the same reason, they became topics of tedious debates: kinship and social organization came to be received as boring topics. Finally, the academic discipline of anthropology differentiated at the same time that anthropologists began recognizing the differentiation of the social systems they were studying. The centrality of kinship fragmented within our discipline about the same time that we noticed kinship relations fragmenting among the people we study. Sociologists developed schemes to examine the processes of change as small communities differentiate and become involved in larger social systems. But these perspectives were never very central in anthropology, perhaps because anthropologists found them too simplistic and ethnocentric.

Anthropologists will never again encounter communities in which almost all relations are kinship based. But an important basis of anthropological understanding comes from comparison, and knowledge about these kinship-based communities provides us with an important comparative perspective for understanding contemporary social relations. Moreover, kinship relations, although they no longer organize entire social systems, remain important in every society. Comparing kinship relations in American society with those of a small-scale society such as Sikaiana highlights the intensity and brittleness of relations within American families and the more general network of support in Sikaiana extended families. But Sikaiana kinship relations are changing, and many Sikaiana people claim that their extended family relations are becoming less important as the result of new institutions and practices associated with modernization.

In examining how interactions with larger global systems affect social relations, I have suggested the usefulness of examining processes of integration and differentiation in the organization of groups and relationships. Small-scale social systems are becoming, however uneasily, incorporated into larger regional systems. Kinship relations remain important but are notable for their differences from the new occupational and bureaucratic roles and institutions which develop. These new occupational and bureaucratic roles and institutions link local communities with larger social systems at the same time that they introduce new kinds of differences within local communities.

Simultaneously, there is often a contrary process in which people within these local communities construct local meanings and activities which unite them into distinctive communities. Thus the internal differentiation within these communities and their external integration into larger social system is accompanied by the attempt to create new kinds of integrative mechanisms within the community which differentiate it from the larger social system.

These issues involve the study of the formation and organization of groups and relations—issues of social organization. Although overlooked in most contemporary anthropology, some traditional concepts in the study of social organization provide an important beginning for developing a comparative perspective to understand important processes and changes involved in change and modernity.

## Acknowledgments

Many of the ideas in this paper were inspired by Bill Davenport, although he is in no way responsible for its faults nor does he necessarily agree with the perspective presented here. A companion paper which covers some similar issues about modernity was presented at the Pennsylvania Sociological Society meetings at Lincoln University on October 17, 1992. I have benefited from the discussion at that conference.

## Notes

1. Writing for the *Encyclopaedia of the Social Sciences*, Robert Lowie (1937:141) defined social organization in the following terms: "Every human group is organized; its individual components do not behave independently of one another but are linked by bonds, the nature of which determines the types of social unit. Kinship, sex, age, coresidence, matrimonial status, community of religious or social interests, are among unifying agencies; and in stratified societies members of the same level form a definite class."

This definition is fine except that contemporary social systems must also be examined in terms of other bonds and units, many of them introduced relatively recently, including those based upon occupation, nationality, ethnicity, and community. Moreover, the organization into "unifying agencies" implies that there are differences between unifying agencies which are also significant for understanding significant social groupings.

2. Admittedly, this is a very crude measure of anthropological interest. For example, "men" has only 43 references and many of them are the result of old labels: "medicine men," "big men." It seems likely that "men" is an assumed

and therefore unmarked category, reflecting the continuing gender biases of anthropologists. "Women" may have large numbers of references because it is the "marked" term; it is considered somewhat unusual and therefore worthy of indexing. Thus, there is a degree of reflexivity in anthropological discourses about "women" which does not exist for discussions about "men," although the study of "men" may have higher, albeit implicit, centrality.

3. Ortner (1984) recognized this fragmentation and made a good call on the direction of future anthropology. By the early 1980s, kinship and social organization were already dead topics, although some people were not aware of it. Beating an already dead horse, Schneider (1984), for example, felt it necessary to devote an entire book to questioning the centrality of kinship studies. Early-Schneider was a central figure in developing the very topics which late-Schneider felt necessary to discredit.

4. I teach in combined anthropology/sociology departments and so have some exposure to sociology textbooks concerning comparative family systems, many of which are quite good, with good comparative examples.

5. In recent years, anthropologists have been increasingly interested in cultural definitions of the self. These interests, at least in part, grew out of earlier culture and personality studies (see Hallowell 1955). Most anthropologists approach these issues in terms of cultural constructions of the individual, personhood, emotion, and cognition (Levy 1973; Rosaldo 1980; Shweder and Levine 1984; White and Kirkpatrick 1985). There is a related interest in social theory which examines the self in terms of groups and social relations. Hallowell's (1955) seminal essay has clear parallels with symbolic interactionists in sociology who examine how the self is constructed out of social relationships.

## References Cited

Appadurai, Arjun. 1990. "Disjuncture and Differences in the Global Economy." In *Global Culture: Nationalism, Globalization and Modernity*, ed. Mike Featherstone, pp. 295–310. London: Sage Publications.

Barnes, J.A. 1971. *Three Styles in the Study of Kinship*. Berkeley: University of California Press.

Barth, Fredrik. 1966. *Models of Social Organization*. Royal Anthropological Institute of Great Britain and Ireland Occasional Paper, No. 23. London.

Benedict, Burton. 1968. "Societies, Small." In *International Encyclopedia of the Social Sciences*, ed. David L. Sills, pp. 572–77. New York: Macmillan Co. & The Free Press.

Berreman, Gerald. 1978. "Social Scale and Social Relations." *Current Anthropology* 19:225–46.

Bohannon, Paul, and John Middleton, eds. 1968. *Kinship and Social Organization*. American Museum Sourcebooks in Anthropology. Garden City, N.Y.: The Natural History Press.

Chirot, Daniel, and Thomas H. Hall. 1982. "World System Theory." In *Annual Review of Sociology 8*, ed. Ralph Turner and James F. Short, pp. 81–106. Palo Alto, Calif.: Annual Reviews.

Collier, Jane Fishburne, and Sylvia Junko Yanagisako. 1987. *Gender and Kinship: Essays Toward a Unified Analysis*. Stanford: Stanford University Press.

Cooley, Charles Horton. 1923. *Social Organization: A Study of the Larger Mind*. New York: Charles Scribner.

Davenport, William. 1959. "Nonunilinear Descent and Descent Groups." *American Anthropologist* 61:557–72.

———. 1963. "Social Organization." In *Biennial Review of Anthropology*, ed. Bernard Siegel, pp. 178–227. Stanford: Stanford University Press.

———. 1976. "Kinship and Sentiment in Santa Cruz Island Society." Seminar paper, Anthropology Department, University of Pennsylvania.

Donner, William W. 1987. " 'Don't Shoot the Guitar Player': Tradition, Assimilation and Change in Sikaiana Song Composition." *Journal of the Polynesian Society* 96:201–21.

———. 1992. " 'It's the Same Old Song but with a Different Meaning': Expressive Culture in Sikaiana Ethnic and Community Identity." *Pacific Studies* (Special issue: The Arts and Politics, ed. Karen Nero) 15(4): 67–82.

———. 1993. "Kastom and Modernization on Sikaiana." *Anthropological Forum* (Special issue: Custom Today, ed. L. Lindstrom and G. White) 6(4): 541–56.

Durkheim, Emile. 1933. *Division of Labor in Society*. Trans. G. Simpson. New York: Macmillan.

———. 1951. *The Rules of Sociological Method*. Trans. S. Solovay and J. Mueller. New York: The Free Press.

Featherstone, Mike, ed. 1990. *Global Culture: Nationalism, Globalization and Modernity*. London: Sage Publications.

Fortes, Meyer. 1969. *Kinship and the Social Order*. Chicago: Aldine.

Foster, George. 1991. "Making Global Cultures in the Global Ecumene." *Annual Reviews in Anthropology* 20:235–60.

Fox, Robin. 1967. *Kinship and Marriage: An Anthropological Perspective*. Harmondsworth: Penguin.

Geertz, Clifford. 1963. *Peddlers and Princes: Social Change and Economic Transformation in Two Indonesian Towns.* Chicago: University of Chicago Press.

Giddens, Anthony. 1990. *The Consequences of Modernity.* Stanford: Stanford University Press.

———. 1991. *Modernity and Self-Identity: Self and Society in the Late Modern Age.* Stanford: Stanford University Press.

Gluckman, Max. 1955. *The Judicial Process Among the Barotse of Northern Rhodesia.* Manchester: Manchester University Press.

———. 1962. "Les Rites de Passage." In *Essays on the Ritual of Social Relations*, ed. Max Gluckman, pp. 1–52. Manchester: Manchester University Press.

Goodenough, Ward. 1955. "A Problem in Malayo-Polynesian Social Organization." *American Anthropologist* 57:71–83.

———. 1965. "Rethinking 'Status' and 'Role'." In *The Relevance of Models for Social Anthropology*, ed. M. Banton, pp. 1–20. New York: Praeger.

———. 1970. *Description and Comparison in Cultural Anthropology.* Chicago: Aldine.

Goody, Jack, ed. 1973. *The Character of Kinship.* Cambridge: Cambridge University Press.

Graburn, Nelson, ed. 1971. *Readings in Kinship and Social Structure.* New York: Harper and Row.

Hallowell, A.I. 1955. *Culture and Experience.* Philadelphia: University of Pennsylvania Press.

Hannerz, Ulf. 1992. *Cultural Complexity: Studies in the Social Organization of Meaning.* New York: Columbia Univeristy Press.

Homans, G.C., and David Schneider. 1955. *Marriage, Authority and Final Causes: A Study of Unilateral Cross-Cousin Marriage.* New York: Free Press.

Jolly, M., and N. Thomas, eds. 1992. *Oceania* (Special issue: The Politics of Tradition in the South Pacific) 62(4).

Keesing, Roger. 1975. *Kin Groups and Social Structure.* New York: Holt, Rinehart and Winston.

Keesing, R., and R. Tonkinson, eds. 1982. *Mankind* (Special issue: Reinventing Traditional Culture: The Politics of Kastom in Island Melanesia) 13(4).

Kroeber, A.L. 1909. "Classificatory Systems of Relationship." *Journal of the Royal Anthropological Institute* 69:77–84.

Kuper, Adam. 1972. *Anthropologists and Anthropology. The British*

*School 1922–1972*. New York: Pica Press.

———. 1982 "Lineage Theory: A Critical Retrospect." *Annual Reviews in Anthropology* 11:71–95.

Leach, Edmund. 1954. *Political Systems of Highland Burma*. Cambridge: Harvard University Press.

Levi-Strauss, Claude. 1969. *The Elementary Structures of Kinship*. Trans. James Harle Bell and John Richard von Sturmer; ed. Rodney Needham. Boston: Beacon Press.

Levy, Robert. 1973. *Tahitians: Mind and Experience in the Society Islands*. Chicago: University of Chicago Press.

Lindstrom, L., and G. White, eds. 1993. *Anthropological Forum* (Special issue: Custom Today) 6(4).

Lowie, Robert. 1937. "Social Organization." In *Encyclopaedia of the Social Sciences*, ed. Edwin R.A. Seligman and Alvin Johnson, pp. 141–48. New York: Macmillan.

———. 1948. *Social Organization*. New York: Holt, Rinehart and Winston.

Mauss, Marcel. 1990. *The Gift*. Trans. W.D. Halls. New York: W.W. Norton.

Miner, Horace. 1952. "The Folk-Urban Continuum." *American Sociological Review* 17:529–37.

———. 1968 "Community-Society Continua." In *International Encyclopedia of the Social Sciences*, ed. David L. Sills, pp. 174–80. Macmillan Co. & The Free Press.

Morgan, L.H. 1870. *Systems of Consanguinity and Affinity of the Human Family*. Smithsonian Contributions to Knowledge, No. 17. Washington, D.C.

Murphy, Robert. 1978. "Comment on Berreman." *Current Anthropology* 19:239–40.

Murdock, G.P. 1949. *Social Structure*. New York: Macmillan.

Needham, Rodney. 1962. *Structure and Sentiment*. Chicago: University of Chicago Press.

Needham, Rodney, ed. 1971. *Rethinking Kinship and Marriage*. London: Tavistock.

Ortner, Sherry. 1984. "Theory in Anthropology Since the Sixties." *Comparative Studies in Society and History* 26:126–66.

Park, Robert E. 1915. "The City: Suggestions For the Investigation of Human Behavior in the City Environment." *American Journal of Sociology* 20:577–613.

Pasternak, Burton. 1976. *Introduction to Kinship and Social*

*Organization*. Englewood Cliffs, N.J.: Prentice-Hall.
Parsons, Talcott. 1951. *The Social System*. Glencoe, Illinois: The Free Press.
———. 1966. *Societies: Evolutionary and Comparative Perspectives*. Englewood Cliffs, N.J.: Prentice Hall.
Parsons, Talcott, and Edward Shils. 1951. *Toward a General Theory of Social Action*. Cambridge: Harvard University Press.
Radcliffe-Brown, A.R. 1952. *Structure and Function in Primitive Society*. London: Cohen and West.
Redfield, Robert. 1947. "The Folk Society." *The American Journal of Sociology* 52:293–308.
Robertson, Roland. 1992. *Globalization, Social Theory and Global Culture*. London: Sage Publications.
Rosaldo, Michelle Zimbalist. 1980. *Knowledge and Passion: Ilongot Notions of Self and Social Life*. Cambridge: Cambridge University Press.
Scheffler, H.W., and F.G. Lounsbury. 1971. *A Study in Structural Semantics: The Siriono Kinship System*. Englewood Cliffs, N.J.: Prentice-Hall.
Schneider, David M. 1968. *American Kinship: A Cultural Account*. Englewood Cliffs, N.J.: Prentice-Hall.
———. 1984. *A Critique of the Study of Kinship*. Ann Arbor: University of Michigan Press.
Shweder, Richard, and Robert Levine, eds. 1984. *Culture Theory: Essays on Mind, Self, and Emotion*. Cambridge: Cambridge University Press.
Simmel, Georg. 1950. "Metropolis and Mental Life." *The Sociology of Georg Simmel*. Translated, edited and with an introduction by Kurt Wolff. Glencoe, Ill.: Free Press.
———. 1971. *On Individuality and Social Forms*. Edited and with an introduction by Donald N. Levine. Chicago: University of Chicago Press.
Stein, Maurice. 1960. *The Eclipse of Community: An Interpretation of American Studies*. Princeton: Princeton University Press.
Thomas, Nicholas. 1992. "The Inversion of Tradition." *American Ethnologist* 19:213–32.
Tonnies, Ferdinand. 1957. *Community and Society*. Trans. G. Loomis. New York: American Book.
Turner, Victor. 1957. *Schism and Continuity in an African Society: A Study of Ndembu Village Life*. Manchester: Manchester

University Press.

Wallerstein, Immanual. 1979. *The Capitalist World-System*. New York: Cambridge University Press.

Weber, Max. 1947. *The Theory of Economic and Social Organization*. Trans. A. M. Henderson and Talcott Parsons. New York: Free Press.

———. 1976. *The Protestant Ethic and the Spirit of Capitalism*. Trans. Talcott Parsons. New York: Charles Scribner's Sons.

White, Geoffry M., and John Kirkpatrick. 1985. *Person, Self and Experience: Exploring Pacific Ethnopsychologies*. Berkeley: University of California Press.

# *Resepsi*: Dou Donggo Wedding Receptions as Cultural Critique

*Peter Just*

Among the many gifts Bill Davenport has given me is an appreciation for the work of Raymond Firth. Bill, who is a wonderful raconteur, occasionally reminisces about his own visit to Tikopia, the site of Firth's classic ethnographic work. On this visit, which took place some decades after Firth had been there, Bill was taken to see a grotto by the sea where he was shown the scant and decaying remains of an offering to the gods of the island, apparently the last offering ever made. "Who put that here?" Bill asked his guide. "Oh, Fossi [Firth] did. Fossi put that there," he was told. I have always been touched by this story, by the devotion of Firth's piety to gods not his own, and by the irony that a foreigner's piety had outlasted that of the natives. This paper is about that kind of irony, and about the ways that we, as ethnographers, may encounter it.

In 1981 my wife and I set off for the island of Sumbawa, in eastern Indonesia where, under the slightly jaundiced but nonetheless benevolent eye of Bill Davenport, I proposed to study social organization and ethnicity among the Dou Donggo. About six months after my wife and I took up residence in the village of Doro Ntika,[1] the annual wedding season commenced. Naturally, I had a keen interest in the marriage process, a series of negotiations, transactions, prestations, and rituals that can begin before a women and her husband are born and last until after they have children of their own (Just 1986a:342–409). As it became known that I was interested in such things we were invited to them with some frequency. I most enjoyed the events just preceding an actual wedding, when a substantial portion of the brideprice (*co'i nika*) was conveyed from the groom's kin to the bride's. These were moments when the marriage brokers displayed their rhetorical talents to great and stirring effect. Inevitably, the groom's representative would try to challenge the amount of the brideprice or, pleading dire poverty, beg for a reduction. And just as inevitably, the bride's representative and her family would assume postures of righteous indignation, relenting "only for the sake of the children, that they be allowed to be happy." Just often enough to give the proceedings real drama, the disagreement would be genuine and marriages would be postponed or called off. But after a while, I came to feel very uncomfortable when the slack period between harvest and planting brought on a rash of weddings, mostly because both neighborliness and a sense of ethnographic duty made it very difficult to decline an invitation and I would therefore have to endure yet another *resepsi*.

A *resepsi*, as one might easily guess, is a "reception" that follows the wedding. It is really a conflation of two events: a feast and, since the 1970s, a program of public entertainment. The feast is, in fact, an event that has probably always accompanied Dou Donggo weddings, and at any rate certainly antedates *resepsi*. The public entertainment takes place in a wide cleared area, sometimes under a large canopy of tarpaulins. Old-fashioned parents will have asked a ritual specialist to propitiate the spirits of the place before setting up the canopy and chairs. Chairs from almost every house in the village and a score of kerosene pressure lamps will be borrowed if the reception is a large one. Invited guests are ushered to their seats, but only after pushing their way through a dense crowd of uninvited guests who surround the seating area, sometimes literally hanging from the trees to get a better view. The invited guests wear their best Western-style clothing; I was once chided for arriving at a *resepsi* in a sarong, even though it was a very good one of local manufacture. The bride and groom are seated on chairs decked out as thrones and, as has been the case in all the day's events, keep absolutely silent and straight-faced, never smiling, with downcast eyes. This, one is told, is because they are shy and embarrassed (*maja ade*). One can easily envision the way their friends and younger siblings go to great lengths to provoke a smirk or giggle, but most couples are able to maintain the approved demeanor throughout most of the time they are on parade. Great attention has been lavished on the clothing and make-up of the bride, usually applied before the religious marriage ritual. Even after dark, she wear sunglasses like the groom, and a fine Western dress or Javanese *kain-kebaya*. Her face is powdered almost dead white, over which rouge, lipstick, and painted dots are often applied. The groom will wear trousers and a Western jacket, as well as white cotton gloves if they are available.

If at all possible, and it usually is, a battery-powered public address system will have been hooked up and the master of ceremonies loudly greets the guests in the name of the bride's parents. He is almost invariably a young schoolteacher, and throughout most of the evening he will address the guests in Indonesian, even though all but perhaps 20% of those present speak only Bimanese (Nggahi Mbojo) with any fluency. An invited notable from outside the village—perhaps the head of a local elementary school or a regency government official—will be introduced and invited to make a speech of advice to the newlyweds. This speech, too, is usually delivered in Indonesian, and often takes as its theme the need for modern youth to live lives of *"disiplin."* If the speaker is prolix, the speech may continue on to themes of current political interest, invariably representing the views of the regency government on some timely matter of policy, such as the prohibition against swiddening. I was sometimes appalled by the condescending and patronizing tone taken by these speakers, primary school principals who presumed to lecture the elders of the village as if they were ignorant and ill-behaved children, though this never seemed to bother my friends as much as it bothered me.

After the speeches, guests are invited to form a line and greet the newlyweds and the parents of the bride, the most honored guests first. The bride's mother keeps by her a large basin into which are deposited modest gifts of money. A few guests may give presents of crockery instead, which are much appreciated since they can be put to immediate use. This part of the *resepsi* may take more than an hour and is enlivened by what, for most of the crowd assembled on the fringes of the seated guests, is the main attraction: the performances of professional lowland musicians hired for the occasion. These are usually a male fiddler and a female singer, who with great flair and worldliness play selection after selection of Bimanese folk songs, often improvising clever and bawdy lyrics on the spot. Throughout this portion of the program the invited guests are called away in shifts to eat. When all present, formally invited and casually attending, have had an opportunity to greet the newlyweds and make their contributions, the music stops. The presents of money are added up and the total (usually less than $50) is announced. The seated guests are served coffee, snacks, and clove cigarettes (the quality of which is the principal means for judging the splendor of the *resepsi*), and the musicians may play again. The bride and groom are allowed to slip away to the nuptial bed,[2] while the remainder of the program is devoted to a *muda-mudi*, a kind of young person's talent show, in which the bravest among the teenagers and young adults present are coaxed by the master of ceremonies to grace the remaining young guests with performances of Indonesian popular songs of the sort heard nationwide on the radio. The musicians may continue to play from time to time throughout the night, until towards dawn, the festivities fizzle to a close.

Of course there was more to *resepsi* than long hours, hard chairs, and the screeching feedback of over-modulated amplification systems that made me come to dread these events. At first they came to stand in my mind as a metaphor for what I saw as the encroachment of Western cultural imperialism on the "traditional culture" of what I had had the impertinence to think of as "my people." Aware of the Western model on which *resepsi* are ultimately based, they seemed to me easily stranger than rituals of spirit possession. More to the point, they struck me as tinged with what I could not help but regard as a self-abasing surrender of "traditional culture" to a superficial aping of "modernity." I would by far have preferred "my people" to be "untouched" by such innovations, or at least to willfully reject them in favor of a "traditional" culture (nowadays we call this "resistance"). As one suspects is often the case among anthropologists, I almost certainly valued the "traditional culture" of the Dou Donggo far more than most of them do.

This first reaction to *resepsi* was "anthropology as cultural critique" from *my* point of view. The rice-flour whiteface of the brides, augmented by lace gloves, sunglasses, and uncomfortable Western dress, seemed to me grotesque, disfiguring. I felt they were heedlessly making themselves ugly to look like Western fashion models when they had so much genuine beauty and grace of their own. I was embarrassed that they so uncritically seemed to be adopting precisely those aspects of my own culture I least admired. I found the whitened skin of the bride a reminder of, even an adoption of, Western racism. I was similarly discomfited by what I felt was the empty sexual advertisement of the bride's rouge and lipstick. And I was also disturbed by the promise of violence implicit in the groom's sunglasses—for in this part of the world only policemen and soldiers wear sunglasses.

I was even more repelled by what I took to be the materialism and consumerism of *resepsi*: the centrality of money, the conspicuousness of the consumption entailed in mounting the affairs, the competitiveness of the conspicuous display and the way it made evident, more than anything else in Dou Donggo social life, the difference between rich and poor. So much about *resepsi* revolved around the getting and spending of cash, that they seemed the perfect instantiation of Donggo's increasing involvement in a cash economy, with all of the loss of autonomy that that implied. Above all, I was profoundly distressed by what I took to be the abnegation of ethnic identity implicit in *resepsi*. In the *resepsi* there was a nearly complete erasure of everything that was distinctively Dou Donggo, extending from the language spoken, to the technology used, even to the physical bodies of the central figures. Is this what *we* were? I wondered. Is this what we look like to them? I hated *resepsi* because they were a reproach to me.

If, while in the field, a sense of ethnographic romanticism—even orientalism—made me more attentive to moribund totemic clans than innovative *resepsi*, it is a common and ancient ethnographic failing. It is easy for us now to fault Raymond Firth (1936) who in writing *We, the Tikopia* virtually ignored that half the island had already converted to Christianity when he arrived. But I also have great sympathy for the gesture he made to the gods of Tikopia, the remains of which Bill Davenport encountered years later. It is the sort of gesture I might have made. Yet I also find myself asking if there is not as much self-abnegation and abasement in Firth's act of piety to gods the people of Tikopia no longer worship as there is in Dou Donggo making their daughters look beautiful for their weddings. If Dou Donggo *resepsi* can provide me with the grist of a cultural critique about Western vices transferred and transmuted into a Donggo idiom, might they not also constitute a "cultural critique" made by Dou Donggo about Dou Donggo culture?

To begin with, I have come to recognize that it was probably arrogant, but in any case patronizing, for me to cast the practitioners of *resepsi* as simply the deracinated "victims" of cultural imperialism. After all, why should I see *resepsi* only as a cultural critique of the West, denying them as, at least potentially, an authentic indigenous cultural critique of Dou Donggo culture and society?[3] It would be simplistic in the extreme to see *resepsi* only as the insidious cutting edge of racism, mindless consumerism, and the wage slavery it compels, to which the hapless, innocent, ignorant, defenseless Dou Donggo were witlessly falling prey. How often, after all, have any people had the lofty perspective needed to see the implications of radically new cultural configurations when they first appear? Surely the Dou Donggo are perfectly capable of recognizing the exogenousness of *resepsi* and, in fact, it seems to me that they prize them precisely because they are exotic, novel, exciting.

The notion of "cultural critique" was made *au courant* by George Marcus and Michael M.J. Fischer just as I was returning from the field. They proposed that

> twentieth-century social and cultural anthropology has promised...enlightenment on two fronts. The one has been the salvaging of distinct cultural forms of life from a process of apparent global Westernization.... The other promise of anthropology...has been to serve as a form of cultural critique for ourselves. In using portraits of other cultural patterns to reflect self-critically on our own ways, anthropology disrupts common sense and makes us reexamine our taken-for-granted assumptions. (Marcus and Fischer 1986:1)

While the idea may have lost some of its currency, it seems to me unnecessary for us to reserve its application to ourselves alone. If *resepsi* could be used by me to critique my culture, might they not also constitute a critique of Dou Donggo culture? If the outward form of *resepsi* seems to be a repudiation of "traditional" Dou Donggo culture in favor of a Westernized, "modern" way of life, why should this be somehow illegitimate? Almost all Dou Donggo, at least in public, seem resigned to (if not uniformly happy with) admitting the inferiority of their way of life compared to what they perceive as the advances of the modern world. Some seem eager to embrace them. Whichever, they all well understand that they cannot hope to compete on its own terms with an outside world that has brought them radios, cassette players, antibiotics, and hybrid rice, and has somehow landed men on the moon. The political leadership of the Bimanese regency of which Donggo is a part has made it abundantly clear that the price for entry into such a world is an abandonment of their "kaffir" ways and surrender to Islam—or failing that, at least Christianity. But it now seems that it is a price they are willing to pay, or if they are not willing, they recognize it is a price that will inevitably be extracted from their children. So it is not surprising that, with the exception of the older inhabitants of Doro Ntika (who recognize that *resepsi* were not aimed at them in any case, and react with benign bewilderment), most villagers regard *resepsi* as rollicking good fun, the height of modern fashion, and as worthy of respect as the schoolteachers who play the leading role in conducting them.

But does this constitute a "cultural critique"? I am not particularly wedded to the term, nor do I insist on its applicability to *resepsi*. I am willing to concede, for example, that *resepsi* are not a critique if by this is meant a self-conscious analysis and reasoned rejection of social and cultural systems of meaning and action; they are not, in effect, an ideological statement. If, on the other hand, we take a "critique" to mean that some sort of comprehensive judgment involving a set of aesthetic and discursive standards regarding one's own society has taken place, then I think *resepsi* can be regarded as constituting not only the basis for a cultural critique by me for my society, but also the substance of a cultural critique by Dou Donggo for Dou Donggo society.

I see this "critique" as operating in several different dimensions. First is an aesthetic dimension, to be read primarily in the physical decoration of the bride and groom. Now Dou Donggo are no strangers to the idea of fashion. Indeed, the easy availability of aniline dyes and a new interest in supplementary warp weaving techniques resulted in an explosion of novel colors and designs in domestically produced sarongs during the 1980s.[4] The whiteface of the bride and the alien clothes worn by both bride and groom, however, strike me as more than just a fashion shift, for they are dramatic changes in form as well as in style. Previously, wedding clothes were either particularly fine renditions of everyday clothes or, on occasion, Bimanese courtly clothes. If there was a foreign model to be emulated, in other words, it was a Bimanese model. With a shift to whitened skin and Western clothing, however, the foreignness of the emulated model is heightened, and it is removed to beyond Bima. This is a complex shift, to be sure, since the lowland Bimanese, too, have shifted their foreign models for aesthetic emulation from Makassar to Java and the West,[5] and in this sense Donggo can be seen as continuing to look to the lowlands for its models. Nevertheless, Dou Donggo models now include virtually no uniquely autochthonous sources, and this, I think, constitutes a rejection of those older sources. It might be noted, as well, that "traditional" clothes[6] continue to be manufactured and worn, frequently by old people, almost never by young people except on rare occasions when they have been trotted out to perform traditional Dou Donggo dances at a Bimanese arts festival. In other words, these clothes have now been reclassified as antique: suitable primarily for museums and tourists. In sum, these changes represent a new aesthetic that explicitly rejects local models for foreign ones and does so by abruptly replacing old models rather than adapting them to new styles.

A second dimension for the "critique" is linguistic. As I have pointed out, the public proceedings at a *resepsi* are conducted in Indonesian even though no more than 15% of the village population and perhaps 25% of those attending the *resepsi* speak anything but Bimanese.[7] But it is Indonesian, not Bimanese, that is the language of modernity. The Bimanese spoken in Donggo is already regarded as arcane and archaic by lowlanders—especially those who have never visited Donggo. The language of autochthonous ritual is, in fact, arcane and archaic; and there are phonemes to be heard among the eldest generation of Doro Ntika that are already no longer to be heard among their children or grandchildren. In this context, the use of Indonesian in *resepsi* also strikes me as contributing to a far sharper generational division than had been made before. To use Indonesian in *resepsi* always struck me as an almost purposely disrespectful and exclusionary gesture toward the older people of Doro Ntika, many of whom cannot understand that language. To conduct the *resepsi* mostly in Indonesian is, I think, a way of saying that this new generation of adults no longer speaks the language of their parents and that they are turning their backs to them.

This concession to the Indonesian national language is also, in an important sense, symbolically a concession to a dissolution of the ethnic boundary between Donggo and the rest of Bima, where Indonesian is much more widely spoken. The dissolution of this boundary has been almost entirely one of Donggo assimilation to Bimanese metropolitan models, and in linguistic matters it has extended even to the personal names Dou Donggo use. As Dou Donggo have found their ethnic identity—associated with three centuries of obstinate rejection of Islam—a liability, the very personal names they bear have become burdensome to them. Like the Bimanese, the Dou Donggo employ a two-generation system of teknonymy, such that a parent is referred to by the name of his or her first child and a grandparent is called after his or her first grandchild (see Just 1987). When we first moved to Doro Ntika, Bose, the eponymous grandson of our next-door neighbor va'i Bose (i.e., "grandmother of Bose"), was perhaps ten years old and still attended the village elementary school. Bose is a traditional Dou

Donggo personal name. When we would mention our neighbors by name to lowland friends, they would often chuckle at such unspeakably hick appellations. A few years later, on my first return to Doro Ntika, I found that Bose was now attending secondary school in the lowlands and, unwilling to be humiliated before his classmates, was no longer Bose but Bakar—a good Islamic name such as one might encounter anywhere in the archipelago. There is a slow but steady exchange of the unique for the cosmopolitan.

Here the shift is more than aesthetic, it is immediately political. Indonesian (Bahasa Indonesia) is the language of education, government, and the state. Characteristically, there have been only two ways people from Doro Ntika have learned Indonesian: in school and in jail. For historical reasons Donggo has long been neglected by the Bimanese educational bureaucracy—village education, though limited to elementary school, was actually more available under colonial rule than it was in the 1980s—and the expense of sending children away to be educated has made education a rare opportunity for the few who could afford it. An ability to speak Indonesian, then, is effectively a form of conspicuous consumption, since acquiring the ability requires greater financial resources than any other investment except, perhaps, making the pilgrimage to Mecca. Not only do *resepsi* reject the language of everyday discourse in Doro Ntika, they do so in favor of language that is owned by the state, access to which is available only through state institutions and by means of involvement in—and dependence on—the cash economy.

The language of *resepsi* also expresses a new dependence on the schoolteachers who command access to it. Thus another dimension for the critique mounted by *resepsi* can be found in the persons who conduct it and the technology they command. The most popular emcees (and that is what they are called) for *resepsi* are local schoolteachers. Most Indonesian schoolteachers are *pegawai negeri*, civil servants. Even the Catholic catechist of Doro Ntika had a kind of adjunct status as a civil servant, since religious education in public schools (for which he was partly responsible) is government licensed and subsidized. These teachers are very much seen as representatives of the national government. Their command over battery-powered speaker systems adds a technological flourish to the political power they may be assumed to wield: technology of all kinds, from radios to miracle rice, is available only from the government or the cash economy, and the teachers are very much gatekeepers to both.

To a great extent, the critique constituted by *resepsi* speaks to a refiguration of the relationship between Donggo and the state and a fundamental re-orientation of the discourse with the world that starts at the foot of the Donggo massif. Schoolteachers most concretely embody that re-orientation, not only because they are the most immediate representatives of the state in local affairs, but because they represent the only means by which people from Doro Ntika can have access to state power themselves. There are a very few young people from Doro Ntika who have entered the military or the police, and a few more who have drifted into the landless agricultural proletariat of Indonesia; the former is rare and the latter, even if it were not rare, hardly offers a better life than Doro Ntika. By far and away the most common route of outward and upward mobility has been to acquire a government job and this has almost always been by means of the teachers' training colleges (IKIP) that are the backbone of Indonesia's system of higher education. In 1983 the children of Doro Ntika included one sergeant in the police (stationed far away in Flores), one unemployed nurse living in the village, and a half-dozen young men who had gone away to seek their fortunes and had never been heard from again, but at least as many working as teachers elsewhere in the country, and double that number enrolled in teachers' training colleges. Their families had made extraordinary sacrifices to get them there and were terribly proud of them. Schoolteachers are thus the agents of incorporation in the state and, for the people of Doro Ntika, the objective of that incorporation. They are intimately identified with the state, too: when Anton, the first of Doro Ntika's sons to become a teacher, died in 1981 while home on leave, his contemporaries wanted to carry his corpse to the graveyard draped in an Indonesian flag; this, they argued, was as appropriate for a teacher as for a soldier. It was as if the state had claimed one of Doro Ntika's children for its own, and they, in turn, were claiming a stake in the state.

The several dimensions of critique represented by *resepsi* combine to accentuate and instantiate divisions in the community that had been absent or muted before. Nowhere are these divisions more transparent than in the emerging distinction in the village between the educated and the uneducated, a distinction that is not exclusively coterminus with generation, but divides the younger generation among themselves as well, a division made evident in the conduct of *resepsi* and the audience at which they are aimed. Similarly, the *resepsi* themselves act to make visible differences in wealth within the community in a way that had not been as evident before. *Resepsi* are paid for jointly by the parents of both bride and groom, which I see as part of a general move to a more bilateral, neolocal, cognatic form of social organization. But *resepsi* also embody the transition from equality to inequality that seems so ineluctably to be the consequence of incorporation in a capitalist economy. Not every wedding is accompanied by a *resepsi*. There may be a few who forbear *resepsi* because they find them culturally too alien, but most who do not celebrate a child's wedding with a *resepsi* do not do so because they simply do not have the money. To a certain extent, to be sure, differences in wealth have always figured in marriages, primarily by means of brideprice payments. But *resepsi* do act to make these differences more public and to make the *expenditure* of money, rather than its investment, the focus of the event.

Yet for all of this, the cultural critique offered by *resepsi* is a complex and textured one, in some ways ambiguous. *Resepsi* may indeed be seen as representing a collective judgment on the part of Dou Donggo communities that this cultural form is somehow at least as legitimate as—if not in some sense superior to—their own ways of solemnizing marriages. I find it revealing, however, that this legitimacy is expressed not by deleting social practices already in place, but by the addition of a new idiom. The wedding feasts to which *resepsi* have been added continue for the present to form an irreducible component of weddings. Indeed, one may have feasts without *resepsi*, but as yet one does not encounter *resepsi* without feasts. And it is not without significance that the grounds on which *resepsi* are held continue to be blessed in advance by traditional ritual specialists (*sando*). Transformations of "habitus" (in Bourdieu's [1977] sense) in Donggo are characteristically syncretic, the kind of layering of traditions and systems of meanings for which Southeast Asia has become so well known. There is, all in all, a kind of empirical tolerance to the way Dou Donggo approach the appearance of the new. The radical exclusivism of both Western and Islamic systems of meaning and belief makes little sense to them. Seeking Western medical treatment seems no reason to forgo traditional healing rituals; invoking the help of Jesus or Muhammed—or of Jesus *and* Muhammed—seems no reason to forfeit the help of autochthonous spirits and deities. Since one never knows for sure what will work anyway, it only makes sense to improve one's chances by doing as much as one can afford to do.

The act of rejection in Donggo is thus a softened one, the language of critique is rarely harsh. In talking about the gradual lapsing of older rules and norms, Dou Donggo frequently begin their statements with phrases like "Now that there is no Sultan in the palace..." or "Now that we have a religion..." or "Now that we live in the New Order...." When, for example, the last *ncuhi* of Donggo, the last high priest of the autochthonous religion, died in 1983, many of my informants seemed uncertain whether he would be replaced. "Now that there is no longer a Sultan in the Palace, it doesn't seem that there is much purpose to having an *ncuhi*," I was told. The office of *ncuhi* was to be *"diwi'ikai,"* meaning "put away, set aside, put out of sight." The term is not without a sense of rejection: a divorced person is similarly said to have been *"diwi'ikai"* by his or her spouse, but even in this usage some nostalgia persists for the happier days of a relationship whose sustaining properties have been lost.

*Resepsi* do not stand alone as the only instance in which the shifts in Dou Donggo society are given aesthetic expression. But I think that for me, and for my friends and neighbors in Doro Ntika as well, *resepsi* have come to stand for the very complex historical position Donggo occupies at present. I want to devote the remainder of this essay to a fleshing out of the critique I have just outlined and of the historical context in which it is being made.

To begin with, the mere existence of *resepsi* implies a great deal. They suggest a Donggo that is open to cultural innovation in a way that, perhaps, it had not been for quite some time before. One must place the cultural liability represented by *resepsi* in the context of a Donggo that was known to the outside world primarily for its refusal to accept conversion to Islam for the preceding three hundred years—during which time that religion was the faith not only of their lowland neighbors but of their sovereign lord as well (Zollinger 1848). Indeed, I was initially attracted to Donggo as a site for research for what I had taken to be a remarkable degree of cultural conservatism, a willingness to resist change. Whatever it was that had enabled this resistance seems itself to have changed, if not disappeared. The reasons for this are both political and ecological.

The political reasons have to do with changes in Donggo's relationship with the Bimanese state. Sometime in late 14th or early 15th century, Donggo was incorporated in the pre-Islamic Hindu Bimanese kingdom by treaty, granting Donggo a special political status. One of the indemnities secured for Donggo was a guarantee of religious toleration, so that when the kingdom became an Islamic sultanate in the middle of the 17th century, Donggo was not forced to accept the religion of its ruler. When Bima became part of the Republic of Indonesia three hundred years later, the special status that had protected the autochthonous beliefs and practices of the Dou Donggo ceased to be valid. Moreover, the new rulers of Bima, both local and Javanese, tended to be "*Islam fanatis*," who had little sympathy or tolerance for Donggo's "kaffir" ways. As Bima began to "develop" in the 1970s, much of what the republican government had to offer—schools, roads, medical facilities, agricultural services—was denied to Donggo, largely, it is assumed by all, because Dou Donggo either were not Muslim or too recently and too imperfectly Muslim. Pressures to accept Islam in earlier years had met a lukewarm reception in large part because there were few advantages to be had for doing so. By the mid-1970s such advantages were more than evident and almost all Dou Donggo had adopted Islam (or, failing that, Christianity, which also has official status with the state). *Resepsi* are largely devoid of an explicitly religious content, but they do participate in a constellation of cultural changes re-orienting Donggo in its relationship to the state, in which greater integration with the state is linked to material economic benefits, all of which are visible in the *resepsi* themselves.

Similarly, the economic shifts addressed by and reflected in *resepsi* are a consequence of recent Dou Donggo demographic and ecological history. Donggo is in the midst of a period of rapid population growth that has come at the same time that agricultural resources for the cultivation of swidden rice—the mainstay of what had been an almost exclusively subsistence economy—have been seriously reduced and degraded. The population of Donggo probably doubled between 1940 and 1980. Most of the growth rate results from increasingly early marriage. Before World War II couples tended to be in their mid-twenties at marriage; but during the Japanese occupation of Bima, women tended to marry at a much younger age, fearing the conscription of unmarried women into Japanese military brothels. Dou Donggo couples continued to marry in their teens thereafter. Naturally, increasing population densities placed greater pressures on land resources, but for some time there continued to be adequate land for swiddening and plentiful forest resources,[8] equally open to everyone in the village. But in the early 1950s the government agricultural service introduced elsewhere in the regency a shrubby weed, *lantana camara*, to preserve overgrazed and over-swiddened lands from erosion (Brewer 1979:86). The weed spread to Donggo, where it took over lands left fallow after swiddening, preventing the regeneration of the monsoon forest. That process was accelerated by the accidental arrival of another weed, *eupatorium oppositofolia*, in 1971. Deforestation throughout the regency has significantly reduced water resources with particularly important consequences for permanent-field wet-rice cultivation. There is now also a regency-wide ban on swiddening, enacted to prevent erosion and flash flooding elsewhere, that includes most of Donggo.

Dou Donggo farmers have responded in several ways. One has been to increase the amount of land put into permanent wet-rice cultivation, but this is a difficult and very labor-intensive undertaking with limited return for the effort since water resources have become marginal. For those who can afford it, wet-rice yields have been improved with the introduction, by the government, of hybrid strains and fertilizers. Another tactic has been to participate in a government-sponsored program using a special hybrid rice that can be grown on unirrigated terraced land. A third tactic has been to supplement rice cultivation with the dry-field cultivation of cash crops, principally soybeans and, to a lesser extent, peanuts and cassava.[9] Nevertheless, households will do whatever they need to do to plant enough of their own rice to see them through until the next harvest, even when growing cash crops is far more economically rewarding. A fourth tactic has been to work around government strictures and swidden. Finally, Donggo has begun exporting people, some to Sanggar district on the slopes of Mt. Tambora where land for swiddening is readily available, but mostly Donggo has exported its young people to schools where they can learn to be teachers, police officers, nurses. Dou Donggo parents, painfully aware of the declining returns of agriculture and the potential rewards of involvement in the national culture and economy, are willing to mobilize almost all their resources and make extraordinary sacrifices in an effort to secure a secondary or tertiary education for their children. Along with accumulating brideprices, the effort to assemble school fees has become the major occasion for activating networks of kinship obligation.

For the most part this is done most willingly, too, not out of simple economic self-interest alone. Dou Donggo are passionate protectors of their children and they are willing to bear almost any discomfort or indignity to see them well off. Elsewhere (Just 1987:325) I have gone to the extent of calling the Dou Donggo "teknocentric," in the sense that children are the constant focus of attention in speech and in action. A man might speak of his best hunting spear as though it belongs to his three-year-old daughter. It is as if the ethos of the society impels its members to speak in such a way as to say, "None of what I am or have to do is for myself; all that I am, all that I have, all that I do, is for the sake of my children." And to defend this deeply held norm, Dou Donggo are willing to give up almost anything.

The result, then, is the kind of cultural critique represented by *resepsi*. It is clear to everyone, young and old alike, that a subsistence economy based on the cultivation of swidden rice has not only shown itself no longer capable of supporting the present generation, it has become essentially irrelevant. If their land can no longer support the people of Doro Ntika, they must go out into the broader world, and if such is what must be, then they had better be prepared to take the world on its own terms. It is for this reason, among others, that the elder generation of Doro Ntika look on *resepsi* more in a spirit of benign amusement, willing to give the schoolteachers their due, indifferent even to the insults of popinjay elementary school principals.

There are many consequences of this economic shift—and of the not unrelated conversion to Islam—that have legal ramifications, changes in the rules governing marriage transactions and inheritance among them. And there also have been less obvious changes that have tested the ability of the indigenous legal system to respond to unforeseen circumstances. Many of Doro Ntika's young people, particularly the young men, now spend much of the year away from the village; some of them are absent for years at a time. In these new circumstances, for example, if a young woman's parents have betrothed her to a youth who leaves the village to attend school, can she be expected to remain as loyal as if he were there? If he has attained a level of education making him fit to become, let us say, a sergeant in the national police, do his fiancée's parents have an obligation to see that she is educated, too?

Finally, the differences in wealth that are beginning to result from the increasing and irreversible involvement of Donggo in a cash, market economy—and culturally perhaps first reflected in *resepsi*—have not yet crystallized into differences of class. But I think it almost inevitable that they will, and soon. If Donggo "develops" the way much of Indonesia and the rest of the Third World have, I think it is likely that receipts from successful cash-croppers and remittances from educated emigrants will fuel a process whereby land is concentrated in the hands of fewer and fewer people, eventually stratifying the community into owners and renters. This is likely to have very profound consequences for the legal system, most likely driving dispute settlement out of the hands of village elders and into the waiting arms of state courts.

Seen in this historical context, then, *resepsi* do indeed provide a text for cultural critique. I still read *resepsi* as a reproach to me and my kind, as a diagnosis of the ills a Western, capitalist, world political economy exports to places like Doro Ntika, even as it provides the antibiotics that save the lives of Doro Ntika's children. But I have also come to read *resepsi* as Doro Ntika's own cultural critique, as an honest and frank admission that tradition is not wholly adequate to the basic task of providing a livelihood for everyone and, that being the case, there is a need to enter into a new kind of discourse with the rest of the world, a discourse perhaps more effectively conducted in Indonesian than in Bimanese.

And finally, I have come to see that the disgust I felt at the irony of the Western roots of Dou Donggo *resepsi* was itself ironic. Irony seems to have assumed pride of place as the preeminent post-modern emotion, a response to the almost aleatoric juxtapositions of a world in which everyone seems to be living in one another's back yard. I find it an unsatisfactory response, an inadequate way of comprehending either of the critiques offered by *resepsi*, a response that trivializes the agonies of a post-local world. To travel half the world in search of the exotic, only to find wedding-cake whiteface does seem ironic, and that sense of irony erected a barrier between me and my friends. But seen as critique, the self-abasement of *resepsi* becomes illusory. The whiteface was more exotic than totemic clans for me, more thrillingly novel for my friends, something alien to both of us. And there is, for both of us, more dignity in the thrill of the alien than in the weary superiority of irony.

## Notes

1. A pseudonym. Research was conducted with the aid of a grant from the National Institute of Mental Health and with the permission and assistance of the Lembaga Ilmu Pengetahuan Indonesia. I am grateful to many people who stood by me and made this work possible, but in this case I am most particularly mindful of the way Bill Davenport propelled both me and my not inconsiderable ego through the process of becoming an anthropologist.

2. Little fanfare seems to surround the actual consummation of the marriage, for which, as far as I could tell, the newlyweds are left entirely alone. While Dou Donggo highly value loyalty to spouses and fiancées, and are will-

ing to go to considerable trouble to enforce it (see Just 1986b, 1990) there is no particular obsession with virginity per se. Indeed, one informant estimated that about half of Dou Donggo brides are pregnant at the time of their marriages.

3. Michael F. Brown (1991) has suggested that Amazonian millenarian movements ought to be seen not merely as "resistance" to Western imperialism, but as having frequently constituted an internal critique of autochthonous society. I draw my inspiration here from him.

4. This efflorescence is documented in a textile collection commissioned by Bill Davenport and assembled for The University Museum of the University of Pennsylvania by Anne W. Just.

5. Makassar was Bima's political suzerain and the source of much cultural, religious, and social innovation for Bima after the 17th century (see Andaya 1981; Noorduyn 1987).

6. These clothes are, in fact, rigorously post-modern, that is, they are a black cotton cloth with a faint dark blue pinstripe made into sarongs for both sexes and a kind of smock and peddle-pushers for women.

7. These figures are correct for the time of my fieldwork. By now the proportion of Indonesian speakers is higher, although I would guess it is still less than half.

8. In living memory the monsoon forest, now a half-day's journey away, came right up to the edge of the village. Easy access to wild fruits and vegetables, fresh game (wild boar and venison), honey, candlenuts, etc., made the average villager's diet much healthier, more varied, and more easily obtained thirty years ago.

9. While cassava might be a subsistence staple elsewhere in the world, Dou Donggo devotion to rice as the only possible basic food makes the use of cassava for more than an occasional snack all but unthinkable.

## References Cited

Andaya, Leonard Y. 1981. *The Heritage of Arung Pelakka: A History of South Sulawesi (Celebes) in the Seventeenth Century.* Verhandelingen van het Koninklijk Instituut voor Taal-, Land-, en Volkenkunde. The Hague: Martinus Nijhoff.

Bourdieu, Pierre. 1977. *Outline of a Theory of Practice.* Trans. Richard Nice. Cambridge Studies in Social Anthropology, vol. 16. Cambridge: Cambridge University Press.

Brewer, Jeffrey D. 1979. *Agricultural Knowledge and Cultural Practice in Two Indonesian Villages.* Ph.D. dissertation, University of California, Los Angeles.

Brown, Michael F. 1991. "Beyond Resistance: A Comparative Study of Utopian Renewal in Amazonia." *Ethnohistory* 38(4): 338–413.

Firth, Raymond. 1936. *We, the Tikopia: A Sociological Study of Kinship in Primitive Polynesia*. London: Allen & Unwin.
Just, Peter. 1986a. *Dou Donggo Social Organization: Ideology, Structure and Action in an Indonesian Society*. Ph.D. dissertation, Department of Anthropology, University of Pennsylvania.
———. 1986b. "Let the Evidence Fit the Crime: Evidence, Law and 'Sociological Truth' Among the Dou Donggo." *American Ethnologist* 13:43–61.
———. 1987. "Bimanese Personal Names: The View from Town and Donggo." *Ethnology* 26(4): 313–28.
———. 1990 "Dead Goats and Broken Betrothals: Liability and Equity in Dou Donggo Law." *American Ethnologist* 17:73–88.
Marcus, George E., and Michael M.J. Fischer. 1986. *Anthropology as Cultural Critique: An Experimental Moment in the Social Sciences*. Chicago: University of Chicago Press.
Noorduyn, J. 1987. "Makasar and the Islamization of Bima." *Bijdragen Van Het Koninklijk Instituut Voor Taal-, Land-, en Volkenkunde* 143:312–43.
Zollinger, H. 1848. "A Visit to the Mountaineers, Do Dongo, in the Country of Bima." *Journal of the Indian Archipelago and Eastern Asia* 2(11): 687–94.

# Chiefs Who Fall Down and Get Washed Out to Sea: The Limitation of Museum Objects in the Representation of Ethnographic Reality

*Miriam Kahn*

**Introduction**

In recent years, the application of critical theory and practice to the museum profession has created a "swelling tide of discomfort" (Washburn 1992:59). There is growing dissatisfaction with old methods of collecting and exhibiting and an almost frantic search for new approaches. Not since the days of Boas and the anthropological concern with material culture have museums so enjoyed the embrace of current anthropological theory. Exhibition, whether in the form of world's fairs, museum exhibits, or staged tourist attractions, is finally understood as it should be—as an ethnographic genre. Several recent professional decisions bolster the new status of museum exhibitions as an expressive and integral genre that is part of a larger discipline. In 1990, the Council for Museum Anthropology was made a unit of the American Anthropological Association. Reviews of museum exhibits now appear alongside book reviews in the *American Anthropologist*. And *Museum Anthropology* has abandoned its former stapled-together format to become an established, peer-reviewed journal. Indeed, contemporary cultural critique seems to have found a particularly fertile niche in the museum profession, perhaps because museums have remained untouched for so long and there is much, both tangible and ideological, to be critiqued.

Since scholars such as Clifford (1985, 1988) first drew our attention to the cultural biases of collecting and exhibiting, this "swelling tide of discomfort" has produced a veritable flood of conferences, articles, books, and "new" exhibits. Many of these document and discuss the museum profession and those involved in it—collectors, curators, educators, exhibit designers—as an outgrowth of Western cultural ideology that reflects our possession-obsessed, power-hungry spirit (for example, Handler 1991; Pearce 1990; Price 1989; Torgovnick 1990; Vergo 1989; Weil 1990). Nearly every aspect of the museum profession has been opened to criticism. Museum buildings are viewed as monuments to Western colonialism and hegemony. Museum brochures and gallery guides, by telling visitors what to value, are seen as pillars of the institution's imperialist cultural authority. Collections are said to represent Westerners' acquisitive desire to possess other peoples by possessing their objects. Exhibit design is seen as a technique to encase and control others, boxing them up in time and space and labeling them for public consumption. The whole museum process is interpreted as providing public space for the safe consumption of dehistoricized, categorized, packaged cultures (Hinsley 1992:18). Even new phrases, such as "the museumification of culture" (Handler 1985) or "the exhibitionary complex" (Bennett 1988), have been coined to reflect the process and complex that taint every aspect of cultural representation and interpretation. The debate continues to rage, although recently some scholars have begun to respond with more tempered rebuttals (Ames 1993; O'Hanlon 1993).

The museum critique has resulted in a chipping away of some of the profession's practical and ideological foundations in order to accommodate the new museology. The cultural voice of authority is being displaced in favor of the presentation of multiple perspectives. For the first time, other people, especially those who made and used the objects, are being consulted and their voices are being heard—in the formation of policies of collection and exhibition, in exhibit labels and live performances, as guides and resource people, and on videos. The museum's possession of certain types of objects is also being questioned and Federal legislation is beginning to dictate who can own what.

Yet, in spite of recent response to questions of voice and ownership, the museum profession continues to rest on its time-honored pillars: collection, preservation, interpretation and display—of *objects*. The power and mystique of the museum object still sits at the core of museum philosophy and policy. Underlying "the museum process," which is Hinsley's (1989:170) apt term for the entire exercise of cultural transfer, is the idea that "the object [is] seen as [a] fundamental element in our cultural and natural heritage" (Van Mensch 1990:142).[1] The Aristotelian notion that objects are manifestations of culture, communicators of truth and knowledge, and representatives of heritage, has not changed. Voices change, videos emerge, some objects get returned, yet the idea of objects as possessable, preservable manifestations of cultural heritage endures. It is the object, taken from its context of manufacture and origin, that becomes our fetish (Clifford 1985), the symbolic capital (Bourdieu 1972) of the museum profession. A recent article (Handler 1992) on the valuing of museum objects (on whether value is relative or intrinsic to the object) indicates the central position objects play in museums. I suggest that if the new critique is to fundamentally alter the practical and ideological foundations upon which museums rest, the idea of objects as possessable ethnographic facts and representatives of heritage must also be challenged.

Here I present a case where art objects and social organization, the two main areas of Bill Davenport's contribution to anthropology, intersect to inform us about the inability of objects, detached from their cultural context, to adequately represent ethnographic reality. An example of carvings from Wamira, Papua New Guinea, serves to highlight the fact that artifacts may defy stewardship even in their home territory. Carvings that adorn a Wamiran aqueduct are created as temporary political proxies. They belong to all and to none. Although a common Western goal has been to collect objects, some carvings may defy ownership, not simply because they belong to the other, but because even the others don't "own" them.[2]

## The *Kokoitau* Carvings

The only sizable carved figures that exist in Wamira[3] are called "*kokoitau*" (a word that has no meaning other than as a referent to these carvings). Four of them still stand today, lofty beings perched 25 feet off the ground, resting on top of posts that support an aqueduct, although these four remaining posts no longer function as structural props. The four are all that remain of the *kokoitau* that were carved (probably eight at the time) in 1948, when the last wooden aqueduct was built. Today a derelict rusty metal pipe, financed and delivered by the Papua New Guinea government and erected in 1977, stands in place of the former wooden one, several feet away from the spindly poles and their carvings that still stand as sentinels from the past.

Each time a new wooden aqueduct has been built by the villagers, which during the past century occurred in 1892, possibly in 1904, and in 1914 and 1948 (see Kahn 1984, 1985), new *kokoitau* were carved on top of some, or all, of the eight poles that physically support the structure (four flanking each end). It is difficult to determine exactly how many were carved each time.[4] Twice, in 1928 and 1977, metal aqueducts were installed by the government. On both of these occasions no new *kokoitau* were carved, a fact that will be explored later.

Each *kokoitau* figure is about three feet tall. They are carved by various lineage elders, all of whom are described as men who are simply "good carvers." Of the *kokoitau* carved most recently (in 1948), at least four depicted men, one represented a double-sided woman, and one a wallaby. The four that are still present are three of the men and the woman. These are of a relatively uniform style and only minor details, such as in hair form, give any indication that different carvers were responsible for the work. The carving style on all the figures is low relief and without much surface embellishment. The male figures sit crouched with knees bent up and elbows resting upon them. Their elbows and ankles were once decorated with cowrie shells, some of which still dangle on the twine tied around the joints. The male figures, with flat faces and pointed chins, display tall combs protruding vertically from their helmet-shaped hair. Wamirans say that the combs, some of which are decorated with a band of carved zigzag lines, are indicators of the figures' chiefly status. The female figure is a double-sided being with two fronts and no back. Whereas the male figures look out to the taro gardens and the sea beyond, only the woman, with her two faces, looks out to the gardens and sea as well as inland to the source of the water. Unlike the crouching men, she stands erect. She wears a skirt and holds up her bare arms (double and appearing like four arms) to grasp a pot of water perched on her head. Although the wallaby was no longer standing when I first saw the carvings in 1976,

*Kokoitau* carving sitting in dry river bed, Wamira.

Site of the aqueduct before it was rebuilt in 1977. Note the *kokoitau* figures on the tops of the poles, as well as the one that fell down in the dry river bed.

photos indicate that its appearance was rather humanoid. It crouched like the men but had a shorter body and head, and no comb.

A solemn ritual marked the consecration of each new wooden aqueduct, an occasion for which the newly carved *kokoitau* were festively decorated. When the 1892 aqueduct was erected the missionaries from the nearby mission station of Dogura, who witnessed the ceremony, wrote:

> On the top of two of the permanent vertical posts they had carved two men out of the solid piece as if they were sitting on top. They had placed nose ornaments through their noses and nice pearl shell ornaments in their ears. They painted the bodies with red paint we gave them and their heads with black paint. (*Dogura Log* 1892)

Today, one hundred years later, Wamirans agree that for each new wooden aqueduct, male figures were decorated with woven armbands, and nose and ear ornaments. They say the female figure was dressed in a shredded-leaf skirt (placed over her carved wooden skirt) with a garden basket slung down her back from her head.

Wamirans give numerous reasons for the *kokoitau*'s existence. Although people often dismissed my questions about the figures with expressions of indifference, their responses nonetheless pointed to the figures' mysterious, powerful, and animate qualities. The following are examples of answers I received when I showed interest in learning more about the *kokoitau*.

> In the old days when we had our own religion people worshipped the *kokoitau*.

> They are not people because they have no ears (although ears are clearly visible, and as indicated above, are even decorated with ear ornaments).

> They watch over the aqueduct to make sure it doesn't fall down and to make sure the water flows.

> At night, the witches and spirits get advice from the *kokoitau*.[5]

> They are carved for our memory—they are there forever.

Men from Wamira village building scaffolding for the construction of the aqueduct, 1977.

Completed metal aqueduct across the river bed, 1978. Note the *kokoitau* on top of the poles that no longer support the aqueduct.

They have no meaning, they are just decoration for the aqueduct.

They are our mystery. Nobody knows their meaning.

They are our chiefs, our *gulau*.

## "They Are Our Chiefs, Our *Gulau*"

Because the main mission of the *kokoitau* is to watch over the aqueduct and taro gardens, brief ethnographic detail needs to be supplied at this point in order to illustrate the convergence between the subsistence system, the sociopolitical organization, and the art form.

The main crop of ritual significance in Wamira is taro, a plant that must be irrigated in the unusually dry climate of the region. Wamirans possess what is believed to be the largest irrigation system in Papua. It includes an aqueduct, first constructed at least a century ago. The aqueduct draws water that originates in the foothills inland from the seaside village, leads it across a riverbed that is dry for most of the year, and transports it onto a large fertile plain behind the hamlets. The aqueduct is used to irrigate the large plain only sporadically. For most of the time, when the aqueduct is not in use, Wamirans still irrigate but use earth canals only. The result is a system that incorporates two sub-systems, or "structural poses," to use Gearing's (1958) helpful term.

In the regular system without the aqueduct, Wamirans cultivate gardens that lie in dispersed pockets in the foothills behind the village. The village is divided into two wards, each with its own leader. In this system, each ward, under the authority of the ward leader, constructs its dam and maintains its canals, utilizing water from a different river than the other ward. In contrast, when Wamirans use the aqueduct the two wards must unite, share water from one source, and cooperate in erecting the aqueduct and in maintaining the canals. Wamira, though, has no village-wide leader nor a common ancestral ideology that unites the village as a whole.

Every decade or more, use of the aqueduct becomes necessary due to diminishing productivity in the dispersed gardens. The aqueduct is built to bring water to the large plain (300 hectares) that lies fallow most of the time. Occasional use of the aqueduct for a brief period extends the fallow period in the regular gardens sufficiently for the soil in them to rejuvenate. Use of the aqueduct, however, causes tension and anxiety for several reasons. First, when the aqueduct-watered plain is used, there is a 30% increase in taro yield, primarily in the form of suckers that can be replanted. Because of the cultural anxiety about what is perceived as abundance, this increase in the abundance of taro also results in more sorcery accusations. Second, there is less water. People must wait two weeks, instead of the usual one week, until they get water. Third, and most important, Wamira, which consists of two antagonistic and competitive wards, must unite. Yet there is no leader to organize the villagers to do so.

Thus, when Wamirans use the aqueduct all their greatest anxieties are heightened—anxiety about producing more food, about sharing limited resources, about working together as one village, and about creating leadership rivalries in a setting where power may easily get out of control. It is at this time, and only this time, that they need an authority figure for the village as a whole.

I suggest that a symbolic representation of authority may be all that is necessary. In Wamira, the carving of the *kokoitau* is an act that creates temporary authority figures in the form of surrogate chiefs and political proxies. Like Gepetto, who wanted a son and carved Pinocchio, Wamirans, when they want an authority figure, carve one out of wood. Often what is communicated in art, whether a carving, a picture, or a performance, cannot be easily translated into words. In an oft-quoted phrase, Isadora Duncan commented, "If I could put my dance into words, there would be no need to dance." If Wamirans had developed a sociopolitical system that embraced a village-wide chief, I doubt that they would need to carve statues for the aqueduct. By carving surrogate chiefs Wamirans have created tangible but perishable symbols of authority in a village that otherwise has no chief and in which power is both desired and feared.

The *kokoitau* are both worshipped and dismissed, are both receptacles of power and mere decoration, seen as both humans and non-humans. They are viewed with an ambivalence that matches the ambivalence about the desire for individual power and the fear of the destructive potential of power when in the wrong hands. Wamirans erect an aqueduct that provides the wherewithal for men, at least temporarily, to produce abundance and establish leadership. Yet they decorate the aqueduct with statues that keep the power away from individuals by placing it in the *kokoitau*, who become chiefs for all and for none. Wamirans empower the statues in order to lessen the power struggles among men. By creating a non-human, yet material, locus of power, men's fears become objectified and controllable. Only 3 feet tall, but poised 25 feet above the heads of antagonistic men, they are tangible and visible, yet cannot be contested or possessed.

It seems significant that Wamirans carve a village-wide chief out of wood rather than have the position filled by a human being. What would happen to a human chief who is needed for only two or three years every decade or so? Statues, when no longer needed, can be ignored, left to the elements, weathered and knocked down, washed out to sea, or even given away.

My suggestion that the *kokoitau* serve as temporary surrogate figures of authority and unity is confirmed by the fact that in 1928 and 1977, when the government intervened as the decision maker (on each occasion designing and financing a metal pipe), no new *kokoitau* were carved. On one of these occasions, in 1928, the *kokoitau* that were still present from the previous aqueduct were removed and given to the government. "In 1928 with the help of the Mission and the Government, the Wamira people made a new aqueduct of steel pipes and concrete, and they gave the two figures [from the previous 1914 aqueduct] to the Government to be kept in the museum" (*Papua and New Guinea Villager* 1957:47). The dismantling of these statues was described in *The Papuan Villager*:

> they gave the Government two images that were on the aqueduct. The village policeman Lionel Didibara went up to Gwagwamore [the aqueduct] and cut the images off, then got everything ready before the *Maclaren King* arrived from the North. He asked the Bishop if he and Eric could go on board and take the images to Mr. Lyons. Then the Bishop let them go and they took the images to the Government at Samarai. (*The Papuan Villager* 1929:6)

## Conclusion

One day on my first trip to Wamira in 1976, as I tramped around near the then abandoned aqueduct and carefully studied the *kokoitau* carvings that remained from 1948, I noticed that one of them had fallen from its post and was standing in the gravel of the dry riverbed below. I knew that soon the season would change and torrential rains would fill the riverbed, carrying the little wooden man out to sea, lost forever. I briefly fantasized about rescuing him. I could save him as a permanent trophy of my fieldwork in Wamira, or an intriguing icon to be labeled and displayed in a museum. Fortunately I was wise enough to disregard my inner Western voice. The next morning, when I awoke with a headache and sore throat, Alice, my Wamiran mother, explained that I had gotten sick because I had gone to the aqueduct and looked at the *kokoitau*. As I listened to Alice's commentary, I was doubly glad I had left the carving alone. If just looking at the carvings had made me sick, I hated to think what would have happened to me had I rescued the fallen statue and carried him back into the village as if he were my own! Or, worse yet, wrapped and packed him for a trip to the United States!

Anthropologists, and especially museum anthropologists, have generally viewed objects as manifestations of culture that can be extracted, possessed, preserved, interpreted, displayed and reproduced. Objects are seen as icons that, if we were only to understand their full meaning, could be our intellectual passport to other cultures. Even if objects in museums are only "cultural fragments" (Kirschenblatt-Gimblett 1991), we tend to read meaning into them as though objects could speak.

Yet the relationship between static objects and the dynamics of cultural reality is, I argue, the real limiting factor in museum anthropology. The irony of the *kokoitau* example bolsters my point. Only when the *kokoitau* no longer "speak" to Wamirans, when they are overpowered by the government and are culturally inconsequential, do the Wamirans let them "speak" to others by giving them to outsiders "to be kept in the museum." When the statues are culturally empowered, Wamirans are afraid to even look at them. It is only through an understanding of the intersection of art and social organization that we can understand the cultural dynamics that empower the *kokoitau*.

For museums, even as they move into the 21st century and respond to the recent criticism directed at them, the age-old problem remains. How can the dynamics of culture be communicated by static objects? There is a recent concern with multiple voices of the makers of the objects. But what about the multiple voices of the mute objects? Museums enshrine objects as though they have one permanent meaning that can be encased.

Museums have an advantage over other educational institutions precisely because they can offer the visual pleasure and interest that only objects possess. The flip-side, however, is that objects, removed from their context, are static. How can an object be used as if it spoke when it utters different meanings at different times? When it can't and shouldn't be possessed or enshrined? If museum exhibition is indeed an ethnographic genre, then we need to rethink whether the very idea of owning and preserving an object might not be at odds with the ethnographic reality. In our reconsideration of museum exhibition, we may have to challenge the very foundation upon which museums rest. We may have to alter our perspective on the preservation, interpretation, and stewardship of objects.

As an ethnographic genre, current object-based museum exhibition seems too static to communicate the dynamics of culture. And, after all, the dynamics are what we are after. Exhibits are increasingly enhanced with videos, performances, lecture series, computer games, native carvers, film series, hands-on activities, and so on, as museums desperately try to create a sense of the cultural dynamics. Objects alone cannot do it. Several years ago, for example, behind a glass case at the Phoebe Hearst Museum in Berkeley, I saw a replica of a *kokoitau*, the only image of one I have ever seen outside of Wamira. Next to it was a label that, like a tombstone, said, "carving from an aqueduct, Wamira, Papua New Guinea."

## Notes

1. At the Burke Museum where I work, much time and energy was recently spent on revising the mission statement, the last line of which now reads: "The museum undertakes these activities to promote a commitment...to the better stewardship of their natural and cultural heritage."

2. There are numerous well-known examples of objects that are culturally inappropriate to preserve (Zuni war gods, New Ireland Malanggan carvings, Tiwi funeral posts, etc.). The famous Thai artist, Thawan Duchanee, intentionally works in ball-point pen on paper of poor quality to make the statement that "art is not forever."

3. Wamira is a village of about 450 people on the north coast of southeastern Papua New Guinea (see Kahn 1986 for further detail). Research was conducted from 1976 to 1978 and from 1981 to 1982. Research trips were made financially possible by generous support from the National Science Foundation, the National Institute of Mental Health, the Wenner-Gren Foundation for Anthropological Research, and the Institute for Intercultural Studies. My heartfelt thanks go to my many friends in Wamira, who patiently and magnanimously helped me with my work. My deepest gratitude goes to Alice Dobunaba, Aidan Gadiona, and the late Sybil Gadiona for embracing me into their family. Earlier drafts of this paper have benefited greatly from discussion with my husband, Richard Taylor.

4. Archival research indicates that the number of *kokoitau* varied slightly each time a new aqueduct was built. In 1892, two male figures were carved by

Kerewana and Lagau of Rumaruma (*Papua Annual Report 1925–26* [1926–27], p. 44). In 1914, two new images were carved by Ambrose Taubobori and Irobia of Damaladona (*Papua Annual Report 1925–26* [1926–27], p. 44). It is unclear from both Wamirans' recollections and archival sources whether these were added to any previous statues or whether they were the only two. Photographs taken in the early 1920s reveal the presence of several carvings, including one of a wallaby. Just before 1928, however, when a metal pipe was installed, only two *kokoitau* were still standing. In 1948, new *kokoitau* were again carved when a wooden aqueduct was constructed, although Wamirans do not agree on the number of *kokoitau*. Some people say six. Others claim eight. Of these carvings, five remained in 1976, although one of these fell down and, by 1977, had been washed out to sea during the rainy season. Today, only four are left. When the most recent aqueduct was erected in 1977, no new carvings were added because, I was told, the aqueduct was a metal pipe financed and designed by the government. The old carvings, though, were not cut down and given to the government, as had been the case when the previous metal pipe was installed in 1928.

5. Seligmann (1910:643) also mentioned the relationship between the witches and *kokoitau*, saying that the carved figures kept witches from crossing the aqueduct.

## References Cited

Ames, Michael. 1993. *Cannibal Tours and Glass Boxes: The Anthropology of Museums*. Vancouver: University of British Columbia Press.

Bennett, Tony. 1988. "The Exhibitionary Complex." *New Formations* 4 (Spring): 3–102.

Bourdieu, Pierre. 1972. *Outline of a Theory of Practice*. Cambridge: Cambridge University Press.

Clifford, James. 1985. "Objects and Selves—An Afterword." In *Objects and Others*, ed. George Stocking, pp. 236–46. Madison: University of Wisconsin Press.

———. 1988. *The Predicament of Culture*. Cambridge: Harvard University Press.

*Dogura Log*. 1892. *Dogura Log*. Dogura, Milne Bay Province, Papua New Guinea.

Gearing, Fred. 1958. "The Structural Poses of 18th Century Cherokee Villages." *American Anthropologist* 60:1148–57.

Handler, Richard. 1985. "On Having a Culture: Nationalism and the Preservation of Quebec's Patrimoine." In *Objects and Others*, ed. George Stocking, pp. 192–217. Madison: University of Wisconsin Press.

———. 1991. "Who Owns the Past? History, Cultural Property, and the Logic of Possessive Individualism." In *The Politics of Culture*, ed. Brett Williams, pp. 63–74. Washington, D.C.: Smithsonian Institution Press.

———. 1992. "On the Valuing of Museum Objects." *Museum Anthropology* 16(1): 21–26.

Hinsley, Curtis. 1989. "Zunis and Brahmins: Cultural Ambivalence in the Gilded Age." In *Romantic Motives*, ed. George Stocking, pp. 169–207. Madison: University of Wisconsin Press.

———. 1990 "Authoring Authenticity." *Journal of the Southwest* 32(4): 462–78.

———. 1992. "Collecting Cultures and the Cultures of Collecting: The Lure of the American Southwest, 1880–1915." *Museum Anthropology* 16(1): 12–20.

Kahn, Miriam. 1984. "Taro Irrigation: A Descriptive Account from Wamira, Papua New Guinea." *Oceania* 54:204–22.

———. 1985 "A Sabotaged Aqueduct: Sociopolitical Constraints on Agricultural Intensification in Lowland Papua New Guinea." In *Prehistoric Intensive Agriculture in the Tropics*, ed. Ian S. Farrington, pp. 683–99. BAR International Series 232.

———. 1986. *Always Hungry, Never Greedy: Food and the Expression of Gender in a Melanesian Society*. Cambridge: Cambridge University Press.

Kirschenblatt-Gimblett, Barbara. 1991. "Objects of Ethnography." In *Exhibiting Cultures: The Poetics and Politics of Museum Display*, ed. Ivan Karp and Steven Lavine, pp. 386–443. Washington, D.C.: Smithsonian Institution Press.

O'Hanlon, Michael. 1993. *Paradise: A Brief Ethnography of an Exhibition*. London: British Museum.

*Papua and New Guinea Villager*. 1957. *Papua and New Guinea Villager*. Port Moresby, Papua New Guinea. June.

*Papua Annual Report*. 1926–27. *Papua Annual Report 1925–26*. Victoria: Government Printer.

*Papuan Villager*. 1929. *The Papuan Villager*. Port Moresby, Papua New Guinea. November 15.

Pearce, Susan, ed. 1990. *Objects of Knowledge: New Research in Museum Studies*. London: Athlone Press.

Price, Sally. 1989. *Primitive Art in Civilized Places*. Chicago: The University of Chicago Press.

Seligmann, Carl G. 1910. *The Melanesians of British New Guinea*.

Cambridge: Cambridge University Press.
Torgovnick, Marianna. 1990. *Gone Primitive: Savage Intellects, Modern Lives*. Chicago: University of Chicago Press.
Van Mensch, Peter. 1990. "Methodological Museology: Or Towards a Theory of Museum Practice." In *Objects of Knowledge: New Research in Museum Studies*, ed. Susan Pearce, pp. 141–57. London: Athlone Press.
Vergo, Peter, ed. 1989. *The New Museology*. London: Reaktion Books.
Washburn, Dorothy. 1992. "Review of *The New Museology*, ed. Peter Vergo." *Museum Anthropology* 16(2): 58–61.
Weil, Stephen. 1990. *Rethinking the Museum and Other Meditations*. Washington, D.C.: Smithsonian Institution Press.

# Affect and Paradox in Museum Exhibits

*Peter H. Welsh*

> And yet...The museum is alive and well, dealing with its inherent contradictions as well as it can, unashamedly against those who would despoil the "sacred cave." The museum is alive and well, jealously hoarding collections and knowledge that could be put to better use, casting only the occasional glance down from its ivory tower on the problems facing the societies that surround it, sometimes pontificating on art, artists and history....The museum is alive and well, sometimes opening up to new technology, feeling hemmed in behind certainties with which it no longer feels comfortable, searching for recipes for serving society and furthering its development. (Rene Rivard 1984)

Exhibitions have injected themselves forcefully into anthropological consciousness in recent years. The interpretation of cultures in galleries, sites, and monuments has been recognized as an important gauge of the exhibitor's cultural values. Museum exhibits are being examined as a medium in which these values are expressed and affirmed. Critics have paid particular attention to the ways in which museums establish their claims of authority through display of cultural materials. Reaching millions of people every year (Wilson 1991), exhibitions rival broadcast media in offering anthropological perspectives to those outside the discipline. Because of what an exhibition concerning other cultures reveals about the society that makes it, and because anthropological exhibits establish or reinforce the exhibitor's values in the minds of its viewers, anthropologists who work in and around museums are struggling to come to terms with the peculiar challenges of the exhibition medium (Freed 1991; Jones 1993; Melosh 1989).[1]

We are all taught that anthropology was born in museums. The next statement in such a history is that anthropology followed Boas from the museum to the university. This may be how anthropology represents its history, but, while anthropology might have abandoned museums, museums had certainly not abandoned anthropology. Halls of MAN from hither and yon, Mummies, Masks, and Primitive Art have all constituted efforts to portray aspects of human experience. In fact, ethnographical and archaeological collections supplied the materials for a long list of "blockbuster" exhibits, typically titled (subtitled) "Arts of the _____" (you can fill in the blank).

Still, until recently, objects and museums were seen by anthropologists as having obvious and relatively fixed roles. Objects carried the semiotic wrappings that stood for their place of origin—that mythical Shangri-la where their "authenticity" resided. Museums had a more ambiguous position, catering to the schoolchildren and the elite. Still, the primary—and presumably trivial—problem was to make authentic objects understandable in the context of the museum medium. There seemed to be little of theoretical interest to be found in museums.

In the mid-1980s, things changed. In the midst of a general re-evaluation of anthropological representations, museums and objects were recognized as marking the intersection of a number of related movements. The belief that anthropologists and anthropological texts could claim authority beyond that of disseminating a particular form of narrative came under critical examination. The idea that objects had (an) integrity that caused/permitted them to remain comfortably fixed in something we understood as their "context" became less and less obvious.

In terms of the history I am creating here, the event that became the turning point was the anthropological response to the 1984 exhibit at the Museum of Modern Art, "Primitivism" in 20th Century Art:

Affinity of the Tribal and the Modern. The critical interest raised by "Primitivism" stands as a landmark, not a beginning, because a significant amount of critical work was already underway when the exhibit appeared (Stocking 1985, in particular). "Primitivism" attracted the attention of a number of writers who were questioning and critiquing the ways that the lives of the "Other"—as distinguished by any number of contrastable dimensions such as gender, class, time, or ethnicity from the author-observer-interpreter-authority—had come to be represented. The critique of "Primitivism" exposed in particularly strong terms a range of taken-for-granted museum approaches to the interpretations of objects and the representations of lives. For instance, then, James Clifford, in his *The Predicament of Culture*, noted:

> The fact that rather abruptly, in the space of a few decades, a large class of non-Western artifacts came to be redefined as art is a taxonomic shift that requires critical historical discussion, not celebration. That this construction of a generous category of art pitched at a global scale occurred just as the planet's tribal peoples came massively under European political, economic, and evangelical domination cannot be irrelevant. But there is no room for such complexities at the [Museum of Modern Art] show. (1988b:196–7)

If "Primitivism" was a landmark, it was a landmark in a shifting topography that seemed to call for a new cartography (Gómez-Pena 1992). The critique of museum representation is but one part of a far wider questioning of how disciplines like anthropology can make sense at a time when many accepted cleavages are being rearranged and while new dimensions of diversity are emerging. Museums' institutional standing as politically neutral, authoritative, and professional is being questioned, while their role in authenticating unequal relations of power has been highlighted. For some museum professionals, unease with established approaches has suggested that museum representation may be in the throes of a paradigmatic, philosophical, epistemological shift. Maybe... But before proclaiming such a self-congratulatory and radical-chic revolution, it is worthwhile to look at some of the components that seem to be at work.

We who continue to create museum exhibitions and see them as important have begun to respond to critical assessments of our practices. Two kinds of response have received the most attention in recent years. First, there has been a great deal of effort directed toward defining and clarifying educational goals, orienting visitors to the "story" or "message" by means of spatial and conceptual cues, and in many ways refining the manner in which information—specific and general—is conveyed. Second, when the subject of the exhibit is a community with living members or descendants, we have encouraged related individuals or those who might be affected by the presentation to contribute their voice and authority to the final product.

The rise of formal exhibit evaluation (front-end, formative, and summative) and studies of visitors in gallery settings as a means for assessing the effectiveness of presentations is a clear sign of museums' desire to establish educational objectives and to better understand the kinds of information conveyed in exhibits. Perhaps the most concrete indication of the investment the museum profession is making to affirm museums' roles as educational institutions can be seen in the recent report of the American Association of Museums Task Force on Education, *Excellence and Equity* (American Association of Museums 1992). But evaluating an exhibition in terms of its information content or ideological stance presumes—incorrectly—that cognitive learning is the primary means by which a visitor is influenced by exhibits in galleries. Responding to scrutiny in these ways keeps museums connected to a pedagogic system that reproduces the very authority structures and power relations that have been criticized (Shelton 1990). What needs to be questioned, instead, is the validity of the fundamental self-description of museums: educational institutions that represent ways of life principally through the explication of objects.

My purpose in this paper is to explore some of the implications and benefits of a different approach. I will argue in favor of seeing the public spaces in museums as primarily social, spatial, and affective. That is, as spaces where visitors interact with the institution and with each other to affirm values and beliefs; where quantities of facts and contextualizing information are likely to be appreciated, but used in ways quite different from our thematic intent. Replacing one characterization of the museum experience with another does not escape the fundamental paradoxes that are inherent in the process of representation, however (Clifford 1988b; Clifford and Marcus 1986). In exploring a new identity for anthropological exhibits of human experience and expression—a "paradigm" to guide our future—recognizing the interactions of paradoxes appears more useful than seeking a unified body of explanatory theory.

## Background

Many critics analyzing museum presentations make a simple division of anthropology exhibits into aesthetic and contextual (or ethnographic) representational modes (Berlo and Phillips 1992; Price 1989:82–99; Vergo 1989). This is a distinction that has been made for the better part of this century (Pearce 1992:111–13). The aesthetic approach privileges a belief in universalist aesthetics over historicized contexts. As Berlo and Phillips note:

> Put simply, defenders of the decontextualization and aestheticization of the objects of other cultures were ranged against those who argue that such a process appropriates objects into a discourse that is about Western art rather than a cultural understanding of non-Western objects and their creators (see also Price 1989; Torgovnic 1990). At the same time, the classical representational modes of the ethnographical display have been the subject of equally profound criticism both academic and artistic, for their employment of a mythic 'ethnographic present' with clear links to cultural evolutionism and racism. (1992:35)

They comment, further, that the art/artifact distinction draws on "representational modes which would appear, by this time, to have become compromised (or at least contested).... Both of these modes are transformatory; neither reflects aboriginal understandings of the object" (ibid). They challenge museums to "push beyond the envelopes of these two paradigms if they are to become truly multivocal."

Challenges to now-standard forms of object presentation in museums and to institutional authority have had a useful and refreshing impact on museum practice. The lists of advisors and consultants to be found in the entries to exhibits, as well as the numerous quoted first-person labels interpreting objects and experience in exhibits and other museum presentations is remarkable and widespread. But it is premature to equate these changes with significant realignments in power structures. The centrality of the institution is not necessarily challenged by presentation strategies that give the appearance that authority has been relocated—whether vested or wrested—to those artists or native peoples whose words are selectively presented in text or sound. The temple is not shaken.

Consider, for instance, the recently opened Paths of Life exhibit at the Arizona State Museum. Each of ten tribal areas has a specific concentration: for example, for the Tohono O'odham area it is rain and water, for the Colorado River Yumans it is "The Colorado River: A Magnet for Many Peoples," and for the Hopi it is "*Hopivtskwani:* Hopi Path of Life." As a museum insider, I was aware of and admired the significant effort undertaken by the exhibit's creators to engage native consultants and to have the themes of the exhibit correspond to the wishes of the tribes who were its subjects. Missing, though, is any indication within the exhibit—or in the accompanying visitor's guide (Hilpert 1993)—that the themes were selected by anyone but the museum staff. Each tribal area is structured around the labeled themes of origins, history, and life today. The exhibit design confirms the sense of overall institutional control by its use of standardized graphics and case framing, with the same typefaces throughout, and with coordinated colors that impose a uniformity to the presentation. Even the respectful touch during Lent of placing blinds in front of a diorama depicting the Deer Dance in the Yaqui area was presented as an institutional initiative rather than a reflection of Yaqui wishes or control. It may well be that in Paths of Life the heritage of museum authority *has* been altered, but the visitors never get a clue. The themes are not so radically different from what might result from more typical exhibit development; nowhere are visitors made aware that their source represents a fresh exploration of authority.

It might be argued that using the device of native voices and native interpretations within the museum supports and nurtures what Terence Turner calls "difference multiculturalism" (1993). Approaches that not only highlight, but unquestioningly accept proclamations of difference as cultural difference reify ideas that cultures are discrete and isolated. So, for instance, in the Times Mirror Hall of Native American Cultures at the Natural History Museum of Los Angeles County, visitors walk around a large case containing Southwestern pottery, with examples from ancient and contemporary cultures. In the middle of the case are mannequins representing the Zuni Olla Maidens, a group of mostly elderly women who currently perform in a variety of settings for Zuni and non-Zuni audiences. The case is arranged such that when visitors face the maidens, a re-creation of prehistoric ruins from Mesa Verde becomes their backdrop. The label says:

> For visitors to the Southwest, the water jar carrier provides a nostalgic image of Pueblo cultures. But for Zuni viewers, the Olla

Maidens, a twentieth century social dance group, evoke a different set of cultural meanings.

For their Zuni audiences, the elaborate, multicolored dress and traditional songs of the Olla Maidens provide an intense display of Zuni aesthetic that speaks to the continuity of traditional values in the present.

In this presentation, the Zuni Olla Maidens—who are depicted as mannequins in a large glass case—become emblematic of the politics of difference, in which "culture has come to serve as the basis both of *imagined communities* and individual *identities* deemed to be 'authentic' in contrast to repressive, alien, or otherwise 'inauthentic' normative codes, social institutions, and political structures" (Turner 1993:424, emphasis in original). The core museum concept of authenticity serves to highlight and accentuate boundaries between cultures.

Barbara Babcock (1990, 1993) has documented the continuing use of images of Pueblo women with pots on their heads from the perspective of exploitation and the creation of otherness. Babcock discusses how this particular image has become "*the* classic metonymic misrepresentation of the Pueblo" (1990:403), implicated in a world of "nostalgic aestheticism, synchronic essentialism, feminization, and utilitarian biases that have shaped the Anglo valuation and imaging of Pueblo potteries and Pueblo women" (1990:443). She notes in passing, though, the paradox that Pueblo women such as the Zuni Olla Maidens have turned the image to different purposes. As a symbol not only of continuity, but of resistance to efforts by the Anglo world to undermine Zuni society, the Olla Maidens take on a role that has distinct political connotations. The image serves to ratify difference not just for the Anglos, but for the Zunis as well.

It is easy to see how museums might use "difference multiculturalism" to maintain institutional control over representation. In response to challenges to museums' assertions of authoritative representations of anthropologically observed, ethnographically described, and authentically enshrined traditional societies, many museums have sought to involve individuals from the represented group as advisors, consultants, collaborators, or guest curators. The resulting silkscreened wall quotes, videos, and such are commendable, in that they indicate efforts are being made to relax some of the institution's control. In all but a very few instances, however, the approach has been to identify individuals who meet institutionally defined criteria to fill institutionally defined roles for producing institutionally defined outcomes.

Following Gitlin (1992) and Pollitt (1992), Turner (1993) argues for a "critical multiculturalism" that examines the processes by which difference is created by majority and minority groups. Critical multiculturalism sees narratives of cultural difference as metanarratives by which groups position themselves for political interaction in an environment of asymmetrical power relations.[2]

In an insightful review of From the Land of the Silk Dragon at the Mingei Museum, Louisa Schein (1993) notes that many investigations of museum presentation rely too heavily on binary conceptions of power and representation. To assume the only active agents in the process are First Worlders who use the museum medium to establish control over the process of representation oversimplifies the dynamics of exhibit events. Instead, she draws on Myers' (1993, 1994) approach in which the multiple discourses about objects and their representations are seen as cultural productions themselves. The exhibit could easily be subjected to a critique of Western nostalgia for anonymous, timeless, homogenous traditions. The Mingei Museum is dedicated to universalist aesthetics where handmade objects are displayed as art. The exhibit presented around five hundred items of clothing, jewelry, and other types of personal adornment from ethnic groups in Guizhou Province of the People's Republic of China. According to Schein (1993:73), the goal of the guest curator (described as a "tour operator, collector, and dealer of folk art") "was to 'document what these people are doing so it won't be lost,' and to 'let them know their work is valuable and that they should keep it the way it is'." Schein utilizes her ethnographic background in the Guizhou region to discuss the agendas of different participants in the presentation of the exhibit: the curator, the museum director, the two consultants from China (both males), and the local Hmong community who were invited to attend opening festivities. She perceives that the motives of the museum are not overtly contested, but that each of the different participants utilizes the occasion of the exhibit to engage in discourse that ranges outside of the institutionally defined themes. The idea of cultural difference is manifested variously in the many discourses that surfaced around the event.

Simply recognizing the art/artifact distinction and difference multiculturalism is insufficient to move museums beyond established patterns. Critics and practitioners alike have accepted as fundamental some principles of museum practice that are worthy of scrutiny. We need to question the stance that identifies museum visitor experiences as oriented toward the contemplation of individual objects in a value-neutral "education" setting. If, instead, we conceive of the public aspects of museums as social spaces where interaction with surrounding, objects, and people is predominantly affective, then the art/artifact distinction becomes moot and we should be better positioned to discuss the consequences of representation in the context of unequal relations of power.

Approaching galleries as spatial, social, and affective incorporates work that is taking place in studies of visitor behavior from the perspective of those who work in museums, as well as anthropologists who have begun to examine museums ethnographically. For instance, in seeking to characterize the museum experience from a visitor's perspective, Falk and Dierking (1992:3) have described three intersecting contexts—the personal context (called affective here), the social context, and the physical context (spatial).

Studies of visitor behavior provide ample evidence supporting the claim that the museum experience is predominantly spatial. The spatial element is in particular contrast with the notion that visitors to museums are there to engage with individual objects. Instead, the museum setting, rather than isolating objects, (re)places them in an alternate context that shifts their cultural meaning and cultural value (Kirshenblatt-Gimblet 1991:388–93). Whether aesthetic and "decontextualized" or located in an exhibit environment that suggests menonymically or mimetically another setting, the presence of the institution is never erased or overcome. Falk and Dierking describe this aspect of the visitor experience in terms of architecture, design, movement, and focus. They evaluate how these factors influence the degree to which visitors correspond to the desires of the exhibit creators, but note that "traditionally, museum professionals have failed to recognize that visitors create their own museum experience" (Falk and Dierking 1992:67). As a setting in which the visitors move through a space in which there has been a conscious attempt to convey information, meaning, and value by careful arrangement of objects, words, colors, lights, sounds, and "atmosphere," we might expect more awareness of the variables that can affect various kinds of communication in galleries. We are continually reminded, though, of how the setting and media divert the intentions of exhibit creators.

Bruner, for instance, has recently described the spatial impact of the New Salem outdoor museum in Illinois. He found that visitors' nostalgic search for "an antidote to civilization" has produced a "soft struggle" between academic interpretations of the community in the 1830s and the meanings visitors ascribe to it by visiting. He notes that:

> Even if interpreters say that New Salem was a commercial trading center, and some do, these words are less effective than the more physical and visual way that New Salem is experienced. The tension between the academic and the popular translates in part to a tension between the verbal and the visual and experiential, and the latter is more forceful. (Bruner 1993:22)

The impact of being in the physical presence of things deemed to be valuable, real, and genuine is frequently claimed to be the special attraction of the museum experience. But the means by which values are marked in the context of the museum environment is, for the casual visitor, an outcome of being in that environment. With the effort invested in creating a sense of awe and value in the museum environment, why should it be surprising that that sense will be taken over by the visitors and framed within their own system of value?

Space is a factor within exhibition cases themselves. Where written work is organized by paragraphs, museum display is organized by cases. We construct boxes to hold things for display and visual interaction, and name that unit as a significant didactic feature. We make our case with careful assortments of words and objects, selectively adding pictures, photographs, drawings, maps, or diagrams. Labels are intended to unite the objects framed by the case around a theme and organize our relationships to them. In some cases, objects simply illustrate associations identified by the words, as when pottery or kachina dolls are arranged chronologically. In other cases the arrangement of objects is only indirectly suggestive of the ideas conveyed by the words, as in period rooms or dioramas. As Crew and Sims (1991:163) note, "the proximity of things to one another perhaps has more authority, more readable meaning than the things themselves." When artist Fred Wilson, in his painting *Mining the Museum,* used artifacts to highlight some of the ways that the Maryland Historical Society rendered minorities invisible, he played on the power of juxtaposition in several powerful presentations. A vitrine titled Maryland Metalwork contained a silver tea service and a set of slave shackles. Looking into a baby carriage revealed a Ku Klux Klan hood, while nearby a doll house was arranged to depict a slave revolt, with the master's family scattered throughout the house (Corrin 1993; Kimmelman 1992; Stein 1993; Stoddard 1993).

Emphasizing the spatial aspect of museum experiences is not intended to suggest that there is anything more logical, natural, or "real" in such visitor interactions with exhibits. In particular, given the resurgence of spatial metaphors in cultural discourse as alternatives to a temporal lexicon (Massey 1993; Smith and Katz 1993), it becomes necessary to be cautious in taking this reorientation as more than having the potential to generate a new set of interesting questions. Space is malleable in the context of cultural performance and the creation of new meanings.

Numerous studies of visitor behavior in museums have also highlighted the social dimension of the museum visit. People interact with those in their own group—families, friends, or tour group—and they are also very much aware of the behavior of other visitors. Work in science museums has shown that family groups engage in a wide range of interactions with the exhibits and with each other. In particular, activities such as sharing a meal or discussing family histories were prominent in the group's apparent agenda. Falk (1985) and McManus (1987) describe how visitors' interactions with objects and labels lead to conversations among themselves that range far from the museum setting. One researcher contacted people approximately a month after they had visited the American Museum of Natural History to ask if the family had done any similar kinds of activities in the meantime. Respondents mentioned activities such as picnics or going to a sporting event; museum visits were equated with socially focused activities (Falk and Dierking 1992:44–45).

These observations correspond to Richard Handler's proposed definition of a museum:

> an institution in which social relationships are oriented in terms of a collection of objects which are made meaningful through those relationships—though these objects are often understood by museum natives to be meaningful independently of those social relationships. (1993:33)

Handler goes beyond the observational claims that when people are in museums they are doing things other than gazing contemplatively at remarkable objects. He suggests that the objects on display obtain their meaning from the social intercourse that envelopes them. The social context of the museum does more than make it necessary to surround viewers with an entertaining and attractive setting that directs them to appropriate museum devised activities. The objects themselves are neither shielded nor immune from the social dynamics of the museum space. Their meanings are re-created in that space so that "the value of any museum object can never be fixed, once and for all, because different people, with varying cultural backgrounds and social locations, will find different meanings in it" (Handler 1993:34). Thus, Handler specifically contests the idea that visitor behavior is solitary, asocial, and contemplative.

Museum objects in exhibits can be understood as entering a particular phase in their "cultural biography" (Kopytoff 1988). Recognizing the social character of interactions surrounding objects on display has been a catalyst for studies viewing them as discursive (Taborsky 1990), reticent (Vergo 1989), or mendacious (Crew and Sims 1991). Each treats objects' meanings as linked to their immediate contexts rather than being fixed and inherent in the objects and their origin. Such an approach connects directly with concerns about authenticity—first of objects and now, by extension, of experience (Crew and Sims 1991; Eco 1986; Kasfir 1992; Lowenthal 1992; MacDonald and Alsford 1989; Spooner 1986). Still, it remains difficult for such possibilities to be directly—or satisfactorily—addressed in interpretive museum exhibits.

James Clifford's reflections following his visits to four museums in British Columbia that present objects and interpretations of native coastal cultures highlight some of the social qualities of exhibits. Two of the museums, the Royal British Columbia Museum in Victoria (RBCM), and the University of British Columbia museum of Anthropology (UBC), are urban museums, and the other two, Umista and Cape Mudge, are operated by Kwagiulth people in native communities. Clifford (1991:232) states "after visiting the Kwagiulth Museum I can no longer forget the questions of kinship and ownership that must always surround objects, images, and stories collected from living traditions—questions elided in majority [museum] displays, where family relationships and local history are subsumed in the patrimony of Art of the synthetic narrative of History." Moreover, "I can no longer ignore the issue of ownership and the history of collecting behind institutions such as the UBC Museum of Anthropology. Nor can I accept without pause the sweeping Northwest Coast emphasis at either the UBC or Victoria installations." Because this approach misses the "density of local meanings, memories, reinvented histories" (Clifford 1991) that are evident at the Umista Cultural Center and Cape Mudge. Clifford observes that, on the other hand, the two mainstream museums also offer something important: a contesting of the national, cosmopolitan milieu of the majority museum and its presentation of native-made objects within a majority environment of value. At RBCM, for instance, objects are presented in an historical sequence, but the exhibits depict interactions between native cultures and national agendas—discussing potlatch suppression, missionization, and land struggles in the midst of the exhibit, rather than waiting for the end.

In asserting the affective qualities of exhibits, I take the position that "education" is misapplied to exhibits. I would argue against efforts to devise measurable goals and objectives that concentrate on facts (as in remembering which Native American tribe makes Kachina dolls), figures (as in grasping the amount of time that has passed since the Impressionists/dinosaurs/Olmecs walked the earth), or processes (as in learning the hydrologic cycle). This is not to say that people leave museums without having lasting and memorable experiences. To be sure, many do. Rather, I would argue that these experiences defy cognitive measures. Questioning the effectiveness of exhibits in transmitting factual information seems consistent with common sense. Walking and standing are simply poor ways to acquire facts. I have encountered labels that take only a glance to make my feet throb.

Claiming that museum experiences are largely affective should not be interpreted as claiming that these experiences are simply aesthetic. The distinction between cognitive and affective does not necessarily correspond to the oppositions between art and artifact,[3] or between aesthetic and ethnographic presentations. This is not to say that such an equation has not been made elsewhere. Sally Price's comments summarize the position:

> For displays presenting objects *as art*, the implied definition of what should "happen" between the object and viewer is relatively constant; the museum visitor's task-pleasure, for both Primitive and Western objects, is conceptualized first and foremost as a perceptual-emotional experience, not a cognitive-educational one. (1989:83, emphasis in original)

Relating to art is thus pictured as non-cognitive and fits with a notion of a universal aesthetic response (hence the justification for presenting tribal objects in an art context). It is not necessary to go on at much length to dismiss both claims about aesthetics. The world of taste and aesthetics is fully embedded in historically grounded knowledge systems (Bourdieu 1984, 1990). My concern is with non-cognitive responses that occur in relation to all types of objects and spaces in the museum milieu.

Again, we can look to Falk and Dierking to find evidence for this affective response to museum experiences from the perspective of visitor studies, and call it the "personal context" (Falk and Dierking 1992:25). The personal context is the interplay between an individual's previous experience, knowledge, and this person's expectations and agendas for the visit. The notion of personal context is particularly useful for characterizing different sorts of agendas that visitors might have, first, in making the decision to go to the museum, and second, in being able to comment on whether expectations and agendas had been fulfilled. The exact nature of the affective involvement with museum spaces remains to be specified, but Falk and Dierking portray the combination of contexts as a gestalt.

Still, the expectation that visitors will increase their knowledge is thoroughly embedded in the museum enterprise, despite the developing awareness that visitors do not acquire facts on foot (Korn 1993; Raphling and Serrell 1993). Korn attributes the continued use of evaluation techniques that produce quantifiable results to the museum's need to justify their use of federal funds to government agencies (1993:253). More likely, though, is that the desire to measure cognitive learning is less tied to bureaucratic requirements than it is a reflection of the cultural definitions of the museum institution. We cannot blame failure to articulate the value of a wide range of informal interactions in the museum space on outside agencies.

Bruner's "soft struggle" is waged over message as well as media. In an extreme example, taken from Diana Wilson's review of the Disney Imagineering-designed Gene Autry Western Heritage Museum (GAWHM), the museum's director, Joanne Hale, states that "school children won't even know they have learned" (as cited in Wilson 1992:57). Wilson remarks that "for other museum professionals, I think the investigation of the processes of learning without knowing at the GAWHM—the relationship of ideology and subjectivity in learning without knowing, what and who facilitates, resists, and interrupts learning without knowing—would be of consummate interest." Hale's comment suggests confidence that the total experience of the GAWHM will produce an impression in support of the institution's goals and purposes. Wilson, I believe, would not disagree, but her concern emanates from a need to document the form that the learning takes. In the short space of a museum visit, presentations that fail to take this soft struggle into account will continue to be diverted, subverted, and contested by visitor agendas that seek affirmation of expectations.

The Natural History Museum of Los Angeles County's (NHMLAC) new Times Mirror Hall of Native American Cultures attempts a departure from expectations in museum exhibits. In this lavish, two-floor permanent installation, not one of the hundreds of objects has an individual identification label. This decision is especially remarkable in the section called the Contemporary Native American Art Gallery. All of the objects in this section come from a collection made by Ted Coe and circulated as an American Federation of Arts (AFA) exhibit (and catalogue) called Lost and Found Traditions (Coe 1986). As Clifford (1988a) has noted, this collection is particularly distinctive because of the extensive effort to which Coe went to overcome the problem of native artists' anonymity and to individualize the artists. When the exhibit's tour ended, the AFA made plans to place the collection in a museum that could keep portions of it on display, and so requested proposals from several institutions. The collection was awarded to the NHMLAC to be incorporated into the Times Mirror Hall. However, now that none of the objects have labels, they have regained their anonymity.

Why should we be troubled by the lack of identifying labels for individual objects? Perhaps the curator anticipated and orchestrated the disorientation that happens when the answer to our first museum question—what is it?—is absent. Such a stance could have interesting results if visitors are made aware that the information in such labels is of transitory significance for grasping exhibition themes. But since visitors are offered no explanation for the missing information, and given no guidance for how to integrate the objects into their appreciation for, in this case, current issues and trends in the production of contemporary native arts, they are left to make up their own stories. On several occasions during my visit to the exhibit I overheard adults answering the "what is it" question for children in highly imaginative ways.

Historian and media critic Neil Postman encourages museums to participate in maintaining a dynamic balance in a society's symbolic environments "by putting forward alternative views and thus keeping choice and critical dialogue alive" (1990:58). "A museum," he concludes, "must be an argument with its society" (Postman 1990:58).

Enticing as such a call to action (argument) may be, can we picture what such an argument might look like? When the Cincinnati Art Museum attempted to engage in an argument with its society by showing the photographs of Robert Mapelthorp, the museum's director was arrested for offending public decency. The initial attempt to offer a native American perspective on the collections of the Smithsonian Institution's National Museum of the American Indian in *Pathways of Tradition* (Hill 1992-93) was received with disdain verging on derision by the New York critics. If the NHMLAC was intending to engage in an argument with its society by leaving out the identifying labels, its society has missed the point.

## Conclusions

Exhibits have themes and messages, but rarely arguments. They have voices, but rarely references. Museum reviews that characterize their subject with words such as "successful," "beautiful," and "impressive," or their opposites, do not contribute to our understanding museum exhibits as a representational form. Instead, there is a need to examine exhibits in ways that recognize their difference and challenge their potential. Bringing the social, spatial, and affective qualities of museum exhibits to the foreground is meant to emphasize the experiential and environmental qualities of museum visiting. In seeking a more incisive and, perhaps, more productive understanding of museum displays, we can consider particular areas of tension and paradox that give shape to the enterprise.

Annette Weiner, in *Inalienable Possessions*, argues that rather than positivistic universals, "it is the paradoxes of social life that contain the seeds of first principles—those duplicities and ambiguities that create tensions that can only be ameliorated and never resolved" (1992:50). The identification of paradox plays a key role in scientific approaches to the development of knowledge. Kuhn (1970), for instance, notes that during the process of normal science it is the identification of anomalies unaccounted for by the established paradigm that sets the stage for scientific revolution.[4] If the paradox is found to be genuine, not spurious, then discipline-based, paradigm-driven science strives to "resolve" the paradox. As situations of unresolvable paradox mount, the likelihood of a new paradigm that better accounts for the observations becomes greater. The new, "improved" paradigm replaces, while simultaneously resolving the anomalous conditions and observations of its predecessor. Hence, the paradigm is "centripetal," drawing explanation, observation, and even perception into its field. Paradox, anomalies, are "centrifugal," testing the edges and boundaries (Myers 1991). Anthropological approaches to paradox are themselves paradoxical. In examining contradictions that are culturally situated (wellness and illness, or fortune and misfortune), or even those that are represented as fundamentally human (life and death, male and female, nature and culture, or even keeping and giving), an anthropological perspective must argue that all efforts to resolve paradox are cultural. Hence, anthropological interpretations of human experience that seek resolutions of "puzzles," "problems" of meaning, or universal paradox must refer to the cultural setting in which the resolution seems to make sense.

"All exchange is predicated on a universal paradox how to *keep-while-giving*" (Weiner 1992:5, emphasis in original; see also Kahn, this volume). The paradox of keeping while giving is thoroughly entwined in the modern museum enterprise. We can move beyond the obvious connection of this paradox to museum collections and contemporary concerns about cultural property. As Hooper-Greenhill notes, "Knowledge is now well understood as the commodity that museums offer" (Gathercole 1989:75; Hooper-Greenhill 1992:2). The mystification and protection of knowledge, as much as the control of things, becomes a fundamental means by which museums engage in interaction and exchange with visitors, as well as with individuals from communities whose ways of life are the subject of display. The ideology of public service, of educating, of giving, is in constant tension with concerns for institutional survival, for conserving, for entertaining, for keeping.

The paradox of using direct experience to convey a sense of otherness also establishes a tension in exhibits. We are mistaken to suppose that objects will submit to the educationally constructed meanings of the museum when so many other possibilities are present in every object and every setting. The educational otherness that museums so carefully construct is contested and diverted by visitors' direct experience. This direct experience in space designed to create a sense of another time, another person, or another place is distinctly different from alternative types of representation such as writing or film. Crew and Sims connect exhibits to theater and quote Cole "theatre, and theatre alone of human activities, provides an opportunity of experiencing imaginative truth as present truth.... Imagination and presence come up against each other in a way that allows us to test the strengths of each against the claims of the other" (Crew and Sims 1991:173). But museums are a stage where reality—couched as authenticity—prevails. We are reluctant to ask visitors for a willing suspension of disbelief, for disbelief is unwelcome in the presence of the real thing. Even Eco's hyperreality asks for a belief in the authenticity of objects in order to offer a kind of experience that itself is then deemed "real" (1986).

The tensions and paradoxes of museum presentations are certainly insurmountable if viewed as problems to be solved. Instead, our approach needs to recognize the continual presence of paradoxes and develop programs that incorporate and highlight them.

## Notes

1. My thoughts on the relationship of aesthetics and social organization to museums is a clear and direct outcome of having worked closely with Bill Davenport during my graduate studies. As a number of other presenters in this volume note, the values that are reflected in museums are no longer undisputed. I think it is absolutely appropriate to assert that the ways Bill Davenport has approached his association with museums prefigured much of the current interest in museums by anthropologists.

In this regard, it is also important to note Bill's seminal recognition of the role of sign systems in cultural studies. Through the late 1970s, he guided me through endless hours of readings and discussions of semiotics, at a time when Pearce, Morris, Eco, or Barthes were less than household names among anthropologists. Similarly, Bill's efforts to encourage me to explore the concepts of systems theory have caused me to be unendingly cognizant of the multiple ways to look at the connections of things.

In addition to considering the institutional context of museums, Bill's connection of social organization and cultural aesthetics led him to direct me, and others, to focus on ways that social relations are encapsulated in objects. While Bill's enthusiasm for the affective potential of material things certainly infected me, he always insisted that our discussions emphasize the place of these things in the context of social actions. This dual approach to objects—as aesthetic expressions and as expressions of social life—has had an indelible impact on all of my subsequent work in museums.

2. In a similar vein, Eco (1990:54–57) distinguishes critical interpretation from semantic interpretation, where critical interpretation is a metalinguistic activity—a semiotic approach—which aims at describing and explaining for which formal reasons a given text produces a given response.

3. See Clifford's (1988a) discussion of the art/culture system for an elaborate set of oppositions that bear on this point.

4. Wallace (1972) applied Kuhn's insights to the interpretation of human systems.

## References Cited

American Association of Museums. 1992. *Excellence and Equity: Education and the Public Dimension of Museums*. Washington, D.C.: American Association of Museums.

Babcock, Barbara. 1990. "A New Mexican Rebecca: Imaging Pueblo Women." *Journal of the Southwest* 32(4): 400–37.

———. 1993. "Bearers of Value, Vessels of Desire: The Reproduction of the Reproduction of Pueblo Culture." *Museum Anthropology* 17(3): 43–57.

Berlo, Janet Catherine, and Ruth B. Phillips. 1992. "'Vitalizing Things of the Past': Museum Representations of North American Indian Art in the 1990s." *Museum Anthropology* 16(1): 29–43.

Bourdieu, Pierre. 1984. *Distinction: A Social Critique of the Judgement of Taste*. Cambridge. Harvard University Press.

———. 1990. *The Love of Art: European Art Museums and Their Public*. Stanford, Calif.: Stanford University Press.

Bruner, Edward M. 1993. "Lincoln's New Salem as a Contested Site." *Museum Anthropology* 17(3): 14–25.

Clifford, James. 1988a. "On Collecting Art and Culture." In *The Predicament of Culture: Twentieth Century Ethnography, Literature, and Art*, pp. 215–52. Cambridge: Harvard University Press.

———. 1988b. *The Predicament of Culture: Twentieth Century Ethnography, Literature, and Art*. Cambridge: Harvard University Press.

———. 1991 "Four Northwest Coast Museums: Travel Reflections." In *Exhibiting Culture: The Poetics and Politics of Museum Display*, ed. I. Karp, and S.D. Lavine, pp. 212–54. Washington, D.C.: Smithsonian Institution Press.

Clifford, James, and George Marcus, eds. 1986. *Writing Culture: The Poetics and Politics of Ethnography*. Berkeley: University of California Press.

Corrin, Lisa G. 1993. "Mining the Museum: An Installation Confronting History." *Curator* 36(4): 301–13.

Crew, Spencer R., and James E. Sims. 1991. "Locating Authenticity: Fragments of a Dialogue." In *Exhibiting Culture: The Poetics and*

*Politics of Museum Display*, ed. I. Karp, and S.D. Lavine, pp. 159–75. Washington, D.C.: Smithsonian Institution Press.

Eco, Umberto. 1986. "Travels in Hyperreality." In *Travels in Hyperreality*, pp. 3–58. New York: Harcourt Brace Jovanovich.

———. 1990. *The Limits of Interpretation*. Bloomington: Indiana University Press.

Falk, John. 1985. "Predicting Visitor Behavior." *Curator* 28(4).

Falk, John H., and Lynn D. Dierking. 1992. *The Museum Experience*. Washington, D.C.: Whalesback Books.

Freed, Stanley A. 1991. "Everyone Is Breathing on Our Vitrines: Problems and Prospects of Museum Anthropology." *Curator* 34(1): 58–79.

Gathercole, Peter. 1989. "The Fetishism of Artifacts." In *Museum Studies in Material Culture*, ed. S. M. Pearce, pp. 73-81. London: Leicester University Press.

Gitlin, Todd. 1992. "On the Virtues of a Loose Canon." In *Toward a Politics of Understanding*, ed. P. Aufdereheide, pp. 185–90. St. Paul, Minn.: Greywolf Press.

Gómez-Pena, Guillermo. 1992. "The Other Vanguard." In *Museums and Communities: the Politics of Public Culture*, ed. Ivan Karp, Christine Mullen Kreamer, and Steven D. Lavine, pp. 65–75. Washington, D.C.: Smithsonian Institution Press.

Handler, Richard. 1993. "An Anthropological Definition of the Museum and Its Purpose." *Museum Anthropology* 17(1): 33–37.

Hill, Richard. 1992–1993. *Pathways of Tradition: Indian Insights into Indian Worlds*. New York, National Museum of the American Indian, Smithsonian Institution. Presented at Alexander Hamilton Customs House, 11/15/92–1/24/93.

Hilpert, Bruce, ed. 1993. *Paths of Life: American Indians of the Southwest Visitor's Guide*. Tucson: Arizona State Museum.

Hooper-Greenhill, Ellen. 1992. *Museums and the Shaping of Knowledge*. London: Routledge.

Jones, Anna Laura. 1993. "Exploding Canons: The Anthropology of Museums." *Annual Review of Anthropology* 22:201–20.

Kasfir, Sidney Littlefield. 1992. "African Art and Authenticity: A Text with a Shadow." *African Arts* 25(2): 40–53, 96–97.

Kimmelman, Michael. 1992. "An Improbable Marriage of Artist and Museum." *The New York Times*, August 2.

Kirshenblatt-Gimblett, Barbara. 1991. "Objects of Ethnography." In *Exhibiting Cultures: The Poetics and Politics of Museum Display*, ed. I Karp, and S.D. Lavine, pp. 386–444. Washington, D.C.: Smithsonian Institution.

Kopytoff, Igor. 1988. "The Cultural Biography of Things: Commoditization as Process." In *The Social Life of Things: Commodities in Cultural Perspective*, ed. A. Appadurai, pp. 195–235. Cambridge: Cambridge University Press.

Korn, Randi. 1993. "Critical Reflections." *Curator* 36(4): 251–55.

Kuhn, Thomas. 1970. *The Structure of Scientific Revolutions*. 2d ed. Chicago: University of Chicago Press.

Lowenthal, David. 1992. "Counterfeit Art: Authentic Fakes?" *International Journal of Cultural Property* 1(1): 79–104.

MacDonald, George, and S. Alsford. 1989. *A Museum for the Global Village: The Canadian Museum of Civilization*. Hull: The Canadian Museum of Civilization.

Massey, Doreen. 1993. "Politics and Space/Time." In *Place and the Politics of Identity*, ed. M. Keith and S. Pile, pp. 141–61. London: Routledge.

McManus, P. 1987. "It's the Company You Keep...The Social Determination of Learning-Related Behavior in a Science Museum." *International Journal of Museum Management and Curatorship* 6:263-70.

Melosh, Barbara. 1989. "Speaking of Women: Museums' Representation of Women's History." In *History Museums in the United States: A Critical Assessment*, ed. W. Leon and R. Rosenweig, pp. 183–214. Urbana: University of Illinois Press.

Myers, Fred. 1991. "Representing Culture: The Production of Discourse(s) for Aboriginal Acrylic Paintings." *Cultural Anthropology* 6(1): 26–62.

———. 1994. "Beyond the Intentional Fallacy: Art Criticism and the Ethnography of Aboriginal Acrylic Painting." *Visual Anthropology Review* 10(1): 10–43.

Pearce, Susan M. 1992. *Museums, Objects and Collections: A Cultural Study*. Washington, D.C.: Smithsonian Institution Press.

Pollitt, Katha. 1992. "Marooned on Gilligan's Island: Are Women Morally Superior to Men?" *The Nation* 28:799–807.

Postman, Neil. 1990. "Museum as Dialogue." *Museum News* (September): 55–58.

Price, Sally. 1989. *Primitive Art in Civilized Places*. Chicago: The University of Chicago Press.

Raphling, B., and B. Serrell. 1993. "Capturing Affective Learning." In

*Current Trends in Audience Research and Evaluation*, pp. 57–62. Washington, D.C.: AAM Committee on Audience Research and Evaluation.

Rivard, Rene. 1984. "Opening Up the Museum." Quebec City. Distributed by author as manuscript.

Schein, Louisa. 1993. "Review of From the Land of the Silk Dragon: An Ancient and Exquisite Tradition of Textiles and Silver Adornment at the Mingei International Museum of World Folk Art." *Museum Anthropology* 17(2): 72–78.

Shelton, Anthony Alan. 1990. "In the Lair of the Monkey: Notes Towards a Post-Modernist Museography." In *Objects of Knowledge*, ed. S. Pearce, pp. 78–102. London: The Athlone Press.

Smith, Neil, and Cindi Katz. 1993. "Grounding Metaphor: Towards a Spatialized Politics." In *Place and the Politics of Identity*, ed. M. Keith and S. Pile, pp. 67–83. London: Routledge.

Spooner, Brian. 1986. "Weavers and Dealers: Authenticity and Oriental Carpets." In *The Social Life of Things: Commodities in Cultural Perspective*, ed. A. Appadurai, pp. 195–235. Cambridge: Cambridge University Press.

Stein, Judith E. 1993. "Sins of Omission." *Art in America* 81(10): 110.

Stocking, George W., Jr., ed. 1985. *Objects and Others: Essays on Museums and Material Culture*. Madison: University of Wisconsin Press.

Stoddard, Ann B. 1993. "Redecorating the White House." *New Art Examiner* 20(6): 16.

Taborsky, Edwina. 1990. "The Discursive Object." In *Objects of Knowledge*, ed. S. M. Pearce, pp. 50–77. London: The Athlone Press.

Turner, Terence. 1993. "Anthropology and the Multiculturalism: What is Anthropology That Multiculturalists Should Be Mindful of It?" *Cultural Anthropology* 8(4): 411–29.

Vergo, Peter. 1989. "The Reticent Object." In *The New Museology*, ed. P. Vergo, pp. 41–59. London: Reaktion.

Wallace, Anthony F.C. 1972. "Paradigmatic Processes of Culture Change." *American Anthropologist* 72:467–78.

Weiner, Annette B. 1992. *Inalienable Possessions: The Paradox of Keeping While Giving*. Berkeley: University of California Press.

Wilson, Diana. 1992. "Review of Permanent Installation at the Gene Autry Western Heritage Museum." *Museum Anthropology* 16(1): 51–58.

Wilson, Thomas H. 1991. "Museums Project Anthropology to Millions." *Anthropology Newsletter* 32(7).